Structural Influence on Biracial Identification

Structural Influence on Biracial Identification

Rachel Butts

LEXINGTON BOOKS
Lanham • Boulder • New York • London

Published by Lexington Books
An imprint of The Rowman & Littlefield Publishing Group, Inc.
4501 Forbes Boulevard, Suite 200, Lanham, Maryland 20706
www.rowman.com

6 Tinworth Street, London SE11 5AL, United Kingdom

British Library Cataloguing in Publication Information Available

Library of Congress Cataloging-in-Publication Data

Names: Butts, Rachel, author.
Title: Structural influence on biracial identification / Rachel Butts.
Description: Lanham : Lexington Books, [2021] | Includes bibliographical references and index. | Summary: "Using the 2000 U.S. Census when respondents could indicate more than one racial category for the first time, this book explores how urban environmental dynamics influence biracial identification. Incorporating several biracial pairings into the analysis, Rachel Butts studies racial integration and the various meanings of the word minority"—Provided by publisher.
Identifiers: LCCN 2021008048 (print) | LCCN 2021008049 (ebook) | ISBN 9781793630513 (cloth) | ISBN 9781793630520 (epub)
Subjects: LCSH: Racially mixed people—Race identity—United States. | Social structure—United States. | Group identity—United States.
Classification: LCC E184.A1 B95 2021 (print) | LCC E184.A1 (ebook) | DDC 305.800973—dc23
LC record available at https://lccn.loc.gov/2021008048
LC ebook record available at https://lccn.loc.gov/2021008049

Contents

List of Tables

Acknowledgments

Structural Influence on Biracial Identification began as a journey in 2006 to fill a gap in the demography literature. Structural determinants of interracial marriage had been a popular topic among demographers for decades. But it wasn't until Census 2000, when "the new race question" allowed respondents to choose more than one racial category for the first time in American history, that macrostructural forces known to influence biracial marriage could be applied to biracial identification. Census 2000 presented an exciting opportunity to extend theoretical and empirical work to adjacent contexts.

However, it wasn't long before I discovered a second gap in the literature, this time within the field of sociology and racial identification. Mixed-race identity, identification processes, and experiences have been a common topic of sociological inquiry for many years. Published studies have largely operated at the micro- or meso-level of analysis. There was a surge in these types of studies preceding and immediately following the 2000 Census, which featured the redesigned race question. Census 2000 has presented me with an exciting opportunity to extend empirical work on biracial identification with macro-level perspectives.

Crossing disciplines and filling two gaps in the literature required the generous assistance of twice as many people who have provided me with intellectual, emotional, and moral support. Craig St. John and Cliff Broman advised me on this manuscript at different points in its evolution, from a purely demography piece to a contextualized race and sociology piece, respectively. I am especially appreciative of Cliff Broman for his steadfast friendship and insightful life perspectives well-outside the context of publishing this piece. I would like to thank Cathy Liu and Zhenmei Zhang for initially (and so enthusiastically) suggesting that this manuscript was book worthy, something that had not, and would not have ever crossed my mind. Believing in it (and me) the way that they did has been my inspiration.

I am indebted to the academics, theorists, researchers, and authors whose work has preceded mine within each of these two disciplines: Peter and Judy Blau, Joseph Schwartz, Terry Blum, Jenifer Bratter, David Brunsma, Ren Farley, David Harris, Charles Hirschman, Richard Alba, Joe Feagin, Steven Hitlin, Scott Brown, Glen Elder Jr., Matthijs Kalmijn, Jennifer Lee, Frank Bean, Daniel Lichter, Qian Zhenchao, Doug Massey, Nancy Denton, Joel Perlmann, Mary Waters, Kerry Ann Rockquemore, Maria P. P. Root, Sonya Tafoya, Yu Xie, Naomi Zack, Ijeoma Oluo, Ta-Nehisi Coates, and so many others. My hope for this book is that it will keep the dialogue that they initiated and developed over the past fifty years going strong.

I am thankful to my peers who offered extensive constructive feedback at professional conferences and coffee shops alike. And I am thankful to the anonymous reviewers whose objective comments and insightful questions over the years really challenged my thinking and helped me make this work what it is today. Most gratitude to my editors, Courtney Lachapelle Morales and Shelby Russell, for having so much interest in the project and believing deeply that it represents a significant scholarly contribution.

I am indebted to my husband, Ryan, who came into this project around the halfway point, and helped me make it through to the finish by creating a quiet, warm, and healthy space for me to write, and rewrite, and rewrite again. I am so thankful for my close friends for their patience and grace, and for keeping my spirits up, especially Sharon Thatcher and Michele McGovern. I am thankful to my mother and brothers for the encouragement. And I am thankful to my dad, Ron Butts, who taught me even as a young child to see race for what it is, and to have compassion for the people subjected to those who don't.

Introduction

Americans are required to report basic demographic information about themselves to the government on a decennial census. Things like age and income tend to be pretty cut and dry. Other demographic categories can be a bit more complicated. Until the 2000 Census, Americans were only allowed to identify with one racial group on the form. How did multiracial Americans choose which box to mark? Did they choose based on predominant heritage? Or based on how they thought the government might classify them? Or based on how they thought the data might be used? Limiting an individual's racial identification to just one group made understanding the American social landscape a challenge.

The 2000 U.S. Census allowed respondents to indicate more than one race for the first time in history. Nearly 7 million Americans took advantage of this option. This figure grew 32 percent by the 2010 Census, even though the total American population only grew 10 percent in that time frame. Either there was a real boom in multiracial procreation, or a larger proportion of the population felt more comfortable identifying with more than one race in 2010 than in the census prior. Likely the jump is attributable to growth from both sources, but the distinction between these dynamics isn't relevant here. Rather, it is the forces that influence biracial identification that is the focus of this book.

What kind of forces influence whether one formally identifies with one race, as *monoracial*, or with two races, as *biracial*? Racial identification is a function of micro-, meso-, and, potentially, macro-level dynamics. I define *micro-level* dynamics as physical and psychological personal characteristics—things happening at the personal-level unit of analysis. This includes things like physiognomy, skin tone, and psychological processes that may link one's identity to one's formal racial identification. I define *meso-level*

1

dynamics as involving immediate social contexts. These things still typically happen at the individual-level unit of analysis, but may be aggregated to describe groups as well. This includes socioeconomic status, family composition, social networks, and so on. Whereas our understanding of racial identity largely comes from micro-level studies, our understanding of racial identification (before this book) comes from micro- and meso-level studies. This book extends our understanding of racial identification with a macro-level perspective. The *macro-level* involves large-scale, environmental and structural contexts happening at a geography-level unit of analysis—city-level characteristics, for example. Macro-level forces (also referred to as *macrostructural* elements or *structural determinants*) influencing biracial identification is the focus of this book.

Different race-gender combinations between parents, levels of education, skin tones, personal interactions, experiences, memories, and various sociopsychological factors can impact whether an individual chooses to identify biracially or monoracially, and if the latter, which racial group a biracial individual selects. Religion, politics, news, art, and social movements also play a role, through culture and social tones. But at an even more systemic level are dynamics like residential segregation, wage gaps, inequality in educational attainment and other macro-level forces. These environmental factors are known to influence incidence of interracial behaviors like marriage, friendship, and crime, but might they also influence interracial identification? This book is the first of its kind to answer that question.

I also explore how the answer to that question differs by race. It is generally well-understood that things like segregation and racial inequality affect different racial groups differently. If these types of structural factors do influence biracial identification, which I'll test in the coming chapters, is the effect different depending on racial group? For instance, although Blacks identifying as also White doubled from 2.2 percent in 2000 to 4.4 percent in 2010, 4.4 percent is still a much smaller incidence than what would be expected considering that the ratio of Blacks to Whites is 0.18. That is, chance would expect 18 percent of the Black population to also be White, yet only 4.4 percent of the Black population identified as also White. Meanwhile, the ratio of Asians to Whites is 0.08, yet as many as 9.4 percent of the total Asian American population identified as also White. In this book, I make the case that differing degrees of impact on different racial groups provide a unique opportunity to quantify the social distance between racial groups.

The term, *social distance*, has taken on a completely new meaning over the course of 2020—the year of the modern pandemic. However, this book uses the term in the classic sociological sense, referring to the distance in social status and standing between groups. Social distance between races, or *racial distance*, is a concept describing the degree to which different racial groups fail to mix. The more racial distance, the less racial integration, so I use these terms interchangeably throughout the book. Although social distance does include spatial distance, in the form of residential segregation, it more broadly refers to the persistence of a social hierarchy (and the intergroup dynamics that lead to spatial segregation in the first place). Quantifying the degree to which different racial groups are spatially segregated from one another is well established (and will be reviewed at length in the next chapter). This book, however, takes that work further by presenting a new way to quantify the broader concept of structural social distance between racial groups. Why does measuring racial distance matter? Just as spatial distance measurements (i.e., residential segregation indices) have shown, large-scale, quantifiable measurements establish a baseline from which progress can be measured over time. This book presents a baseline for measuring racial distance/integration.

An example may help clarify this concept. Distinctions across metropolitan areas hint that underlying structural differences may indeed be affecting the likelihood of biracial identification. Drastic variation among Blacks identifying as also White in the 2010 Census ranges from 0.6 percent in Jackson, Mississippi, to 42.2 percent in Coeur d'Alene, Idaho. Meanwhile, I find less drastic variation across cities among Asians identifying as also White. Why might biracial incidence with Whites differ between Blacks and Asians? If structural influences such as residential segregation and educational inequality influence interracial identification, then the relative magnitude of that influence is arguably a proxy for racial distance. This preliminarily suggests that racial distance between Whites and each of these two racial minority groups can be quantified, giving policy makers a new opportunity to measure progress (or lack thereof) on racial distancing over time.

What does "making progress on racial distance" even mean? If racial distance refers to the degree to which different racial groups mix in society, making progress on racial distance means greater interracial mixing. And by interracial mixing, I'm not referring to assimilation, or any other concept associated with conforming the rich variation in our nation's cultural fabric to the White standard. Instead, I mean that where Whites are, Blacks are, whether that's in schools, neighborhoods, MBA programs, high-rise offices, board rooms, or living rooms. It means destroying boundaries that perpetuate a social hierarchy in America where one's social standing is a function of one's skin color. But it cuts even deeper than that. It means addressing deep, systemic psychological and cultural belief systems that have such horrid consequences that well-meaning initiatives driving toward things like equitable wages almost seem superficial.

Racial distance in America is a clear sign of a hard-wired institutional social problem with severe consequences. For example, the cases of police brutality against unarmed Blacks are astounding. And it's disgusting. Blacks are disproportionately being restrained, beaten, and dying at the hands of police officers who are rarely brought to justice. (See Coats [2015] and Oluo [2018] for powerful discussions of police brutality against Blacks.) The Black Lives Matter (BLM) movement was founded in response to these attacks. By protesting racially motivated violence against Blacks, BLM aims to "eradicate White supremacy" (Garza, Cullors and Tometi, 2020).

Full eradication may not be possible (Banaji and Greenwald 2016). Police brutality is but one of many symptoms of a deeper plague on our nation, and every one of us is symptomatic. Perhaps the greatest of American tragedies is the persistent effect of slavery on contemporary American culture—a curse from which we collectively may never fully recover. But as with many incurable diseases, there is reason to believe we can not only manage symptoms, we can outsmart a disease which cannot be cured. Winning immediate improvements through BLM, reframing our national narrative through The 1619 Project, institutionalizing diversity & inclusion (D&I) strategies in corporations and communities, increasing our awareness of interpersonal blind spots and unconscious biases, reducing subjectivity from judgments, prioritizing culture-add over culture-fit in hiring practices, and considering reparations are just some of the many ways Americans have been trying to "outsmart the machine" in 2020.

Racial distance is an indicator of a really serious social problem, so being able to quantitatively measure and track it is critical. Historically, *interracial marriage* has been referenced as a symbol of racial integration in the intergroup relations literature. In this book, I propose *interracial identification* as a much sharper racial integration proxy after first understanding what structural factors influence these phenomena. Do macrostructural forces known to influence biracial marriage also influence biracial identification? Borrowing from prior theoretical and empirical scholarship on intergroup relations, this book explores how urban structural factors affecting mixed-race marriage also affect mixed-race identification. And by understanding what environmental factors correlate with mixed-race people,[1] I shed light on what factors are perpetuating racial distance.

THEORETICAL FRAMEWORK FOR THE STUDY OF INTERGROUP RELATIONS

People naturally gravitate toward others like them. They tend to seek similar others for friendships and romantic relationships alike. This is unconscious human nature, not necessarily a sign of an overt failure to be inclusive. It can be observed at a young age when little boys play with boys, and little girls play with girls in nursery school. Even when "opposites attract" extrinsically, those individuals tend to have much in common intrinsically. But some demographic lines are bolder than others, and interracial marriage has been of interest to demographers over the decades for this reason.

Peter Blau's macrostructural theory of intergroup relations was introduced in 1977. Blau used the term *relations* because the theory can be applied to any type of interpersonal contact (e.g., friendships, marriages, and even interpersonal crime), although the theory is most frequently applied to marriage. He uses the term *intergroup* because the theory can be applied to any type of demographic delineation (e.g., age, social class, education, religion), although race is by far the most frequent application of the theory.

Because people tend to prefer demographically similar others, sometimes referred to as *in-group others*, the theory's intent is to explain why people sometimes choose to have *intergroup relations*[2]—relationships with someone from an *out-group*, to use Blau's language. Now, people are members of all sorts of groups (e.g., social class, religion, race). But, one demographic slice tends to be more salient than others, even if we're unconscious of it. This is especially true when it comes to marriage. In some cases, the most salient demographic slice is religious background, and shared race and class are less critical to a socially supported marriage so long as religious values are shared. In other cases, social class dominates. Blau's interest isn't in the group definition or even in the people themselves, but rather in identifying the environmental conditions that facilitate the likelihood of marrying outside one's most salient demographic group, whatever that may be.

But let's start with what must be true for two people to marry in the first place, regardless of whether they marry "in" or "out." Two very basic conditions must be met for consenting adults to wed in the United States (although there are exceptions, such as in the case of arranged marriages). The two persons must have crossed paths (in order to meet each other) and have a preference for each other (in order to willingly enter into a contractual union). The opportunity for contact, at the very least, and preference for the other person, secondarily, are essential marriage requirements in a free state. As explained earlier, it's natural to prefer similar others. And it's common (whether right or wrong) to live in closer proximity to similar others than to dissimilar others. Therefore, *in-marriage* (short for in-group marriage, meaning a union between two people who have the most salient demographic in common), is the norm. *Out-marriage*, often called *inter-marriage*,[3] is where things get interesting.

The basic premise of Blau's theory contends that the probability of intergroup relations (e.g., out-marriage) depends on key environmental factors evident in a city's social structure. These environmental factors govern social opportunities. That is, they heavily influence the likelihood that two people will encounter one another, or prefer one another once they do. Blau identifies three, inter-related factors affecting the likelihood of out-marriage.

First, the chances of developing a relationship with someone from a different demographic group are dependent on meaningful exposure to members of that group. That sounds simple enough, but it needs to be unpacked. Exposure to others outside one's own group is more common when groups are heterogenous. A demographic group (e.g., Asian Americans) is *heterogeneous* when its members are well-distributed across other demographic slices (e.g., social class, religion) where exposure to other groups is inevitable and relationships with members of these groups become more likely. (This is in opposition to *homogeneous* groups whose members are not well-distributed across other demographic slices. Since homogeneous groups have less overlap with other groups, members tend to have a lot of different dynamics in common with members of their own group, and little in common with members of other groups.)

Furthermore, the more things people have in common, the less the one unshared characteristic matters frankly. For example, two people that grew up in the same neighborhood, went to the same school, and have similar economic, religious, and political backgrounds probably have similar value systems even if they are racially different. One might even say they have more in common than not in common. In fact, the more heterogenous the group, the less likely individuals have much in common with members of their own group beyond the demographic label itself. Relationship development is facilitated by having things in common, and the more things in common, the less relevant a racial difference becomes.

Whereas this first key factor is about meaningful exposure to similar-others *outside* the group, the second key factor is about the availability of similar-others *inside* the group. As salient as race is in America, two people would probably not wed if all they had in common was race. But if they not only had race in common but also had education and other types of status in common, they may. If there are ample similar-status options within one's dominant demographic group, in-marriage is more likely than out-marriage because people prefer similar-others. But when there are few in-group individuals of otherwise similar status on other characteristics beyond one's dominant demographic, there are proportionately more out-group individuals of otherwise similar status to choose from. This concept is really about equality. When equality between racial groups is low, minority group individuals at the upper end of the socioeconomic spectrum are more likely to look outside their group for a partner of similar standing because options within the group are so limited in number.

A third element, group size, affects the likelihood of developing a relationship with someone from a different group, through its impact tends to be blurred with the two other key factors covered above. For example, numerically large minority groups tend to have limited contact and commonalities with other groups (Blau 1980; Castles and Miller 2003; Qian, Glick and Batson 2012; Sassen 2001, 2006; Waters 1999). This is a function of the group becoming delineated and homogenized through geographic and social segregation (Blalock 1967; Massey and Denton 1993; Waters 1999; Wilson 1980). So, the chances of developing relationships outside the group are low because both contact and mutual preference are reduced.

However, there are some cities that are more advanced in their journey toward racial equality. These areas have numerically large minority groups that are more heterogenous than their counterparts in cities suffering from greater racial inequality. As explained earlier, heterogenous groups are more likely to out-marry than homogeneous groups. But if the heterogeneous group is large, there are ample opportunities for developing relationships with members of similar status on other demographic characteristics within one's dominant demographic. Therefore, group size can actually trump the effect of group heterogeneity on the likelihood to out-marry. In summary, large groups tend to be homogenous and therefore are more likely to in-marry than out-marry. And even when they're heterogeneous, they'll still be more likely to in-marry than out-marry but for a different reason. Meanwhile, small groups (which are rarely homogenous by their very nature) are more likely to out-marry, not just because of their heterogeneity but also because the group size limits in-group options. Even in cases where small groups are homogenous, their members are more likely to out-marry, again, because the group size limits in-group options. In both cases, the theory maintains that intergroup relations are less likely among members of large groups and more likely among members of small groups.

In summary, cities where the racial minority group has greater exposure to the majority group have higher incidence of intergroup relations. And cities with smaller racial minority groups tend to have higher incidence of intergroup relations. But cities with greater equality between groups actually have lower incidence of intergroup relations because people presumably prefer relations within their own group when there is an adequately sized selection pool of same-status suitors. An examination of these processes depends on the comparison of groups unevenly distributed across a social hierarchy. The theory lends itself to "race" as the demographic characteristic defining group membership. The interracial phenomena examined through this lens in the past include interracial contact, conflict/crime, friendship and most often, marriage.

GUESS WHO'S COMING TO DINNER

Interracial marriage has been a popular topic for demographers for many decades. There is considerable work published in this area across three different perspectives: exchange, assimilationist, and opportunity-structure. Here I present a brief landscape view of intermarriage research representing the opportunity-structure perspective (i.e., macrostructural theory of intergroup relations) so that readers can understand the general approach, as well as identify some gaps in the approach, which I hope to resolve in the chapters that follow.

Peter Blau introduced his macrostructural theory of intergroup relations in 1977. His first full test of the theory accompanied a slight theoretical revision a few years later (Blau and Schwartz 1984). Blau and colleagues then retested the theory in different ways, experimenting with different ways to operationalize the theory's postulates and constructs. These strategic exercises helped refine Blau's final version of the theory published in 1994.

A good number of macrostructural perspective intermarriage studies were produced in the period from 1984 to 1994, followed by a resurgence post-1994. Most of these analyze just one racial pairing at a time, such as Black-White intermarriage (Fitzpatrick and Hwang 1992), Asian-White (Hwang, Saenz and Aguirre 1997), and Hispanic-White (Anderson and Saenz 1994; Lichter et al. 2007). Others investigate interracial pairings more generally, such as White and all other race couples (Blum 1984; Hwang, Saenz and Aguirre 1997; South and Messner 1986), non-White and all other race couples (South and Messner 1986), Asian and all other race couples (Hwang, Saenz and Aguirre 1994, 1997), or simply look at all intermarriage without specifying the groups at all (Blau, Beeker and Fitzpatrick 1984; South and Messner 1986). This makes comparisons between racial groups difficult. Only a handful of studies have executed a multi-group design using specific racial groups in a way that group differences in the United States can easily be identified. Two clean examples include Qian (1999) who compares Black-White, Asian-White, and Hispanic-White intermarriage, and Heaton and Jacobson (2000) who compare intermarriage between Whites, Blacks, Asians, and Hispanics. Whereas Qian (1999) examines three different racial minority groups intermarrying with Whites, the advantage of the Heaton and Jacobson piece is that inter-minority intermarriage is also investigated. This work represents significant contribution to the literature.

There is one especially unique contribution that I'd like to highlight here, despite it not being an intermarriage study. Hwang and Xi (2008) use Blau's framework and the accompanying empiricism on interracial marriage to see if the same things that influence the likelihood people from different races will intermarry also influence the likelihood people from different language backgrounds will become fluent in a common language. As opposed to *inter-marriage* as an outcome variable, this study uses *inter-language* (as I'll call it here) as an outcome variable. It may be a bit of a niche topic; however, this study's design is particularly relevant to what I hope to accomplish with this book for two reasons. First, it extends the theory beyond the context of marriage (and friendship and crime) to a new context not previously applied to the theory. Specifically, it extends the theory of intergroup relations beyond intermarriage to inter-language on the basis that "the structural factors affecting intergroup relations should also affect the ability for members of different groups to communicate using a common language" (p. 1079). Similarly, my study hopes to extend the theory of intergroup relations beyond intermarriage to *inter-identification* (as I'll call it here) on the same basis: the same structural factors affecting interracial relationships should also affect the likelihood of interracial progeny. Second, Hwang and Xi extend Blau framework empiricism beyond the likelihood that persons from two different races will have relations, to the likelihood that a single person will learn to speak two different languages. Similarly, I test the extent to which macrostructural theory can be extended beyond explaining the likelihood persons from two different races will have relations, to the likelihood a single person will identify with two different races.

In conclusion, what most of these empirical pieces have in common is they examine the impact of segregation, inequality, and group size on different racial and ethnic groups within the framework of Blau's theory. They use census data (between 1960 and 2000) to identify and explain variation across metropolitan statistical areas (MSAs). Many of them cite the quantitative strength of the relationships tested (i.e., R^2), making them easy to compare to the results of others. I leverage these strong suits in my own analytic design. Meanwhile, there are few studies that compare and contrast different racial pairings and even fewer that investigate double-minority models to better understand inter-minority dynamics. My analytic design overcomes these shortcomings in an effort to strengthen our understanding and measurement of racial integration.

FROM INTERRACIAL MARRIAGE TO INTERRACIAL IDENTIFICATION

As mentioned, Peter Blau introduced his macrostructural theory in 1977. His first full test of the theory accompanied a slight theoretical revision a few years later (Blau and Schwartz 1984). Blau and colleagues then retested the theory in different ways (Blau, Beeker and Fitzpatrick 1984; Blau and Blau 1982; Blau, Blum and Schwartz 1982; Blum 1984, 1985; Rytina et al. 1988).

Other empiricists followed suit (Anderson and Saenz 1994; Fitzpatrick and Hwang 1992; Hwang, Saenz and Aguirre 1994; Messner and South 1986; Sampson 1984; Skvoretz 1983, 1990; South and Messner 1986; Tucker and Mitchell-Kernan 1990). Blau revised and simplified the theory in 1994. Additional empiricism followed (Heaton and Jacobson 2000; Hwang, Saenz and Aguirre 1997) but has tapered in recent years, perhaps due to saturation from generally strong empirical support within the context of interracial marriage, and occasionally other topics involving interracial contact.

But might Blau's theory apply to interracial identification? And if it does, wouldn't interracial people be a stronger and less volatile proxy for racial integration than interracial relationships now that interraciality can be quantitatively measured on a national scale? To evaluate whether social forces known to influence interracial relationships (like marriage) also influence interracial identification, I examine the impact of three key environmental factors on biracial identification incidence across 363 metropolitan areas in the continental United States.

The ultimate source of racial identification aggregated at the city level in the United States is the census. Respondents could self-identify with as many racial categories as desired on both the 2000 Census and the 2010 Census. I first tested my analysis using 2000 Census data (Butts 2008). After promising results, I repeat the work here using the 2010 Census and some minor methodological refinements. The decennial census also provides data for most of the explanatory variables outlined in the theory. I obtained remaining variables not available through the decennial census from the Census Bureau's American Community Survey (ACS).

Why do some cities have higher proportions of biracial identification than others? To answer this question, I borrow from a macrostructural theory of intergroup relations and its accompanying empirical scholarship on the structural determinants of interracial marriage. I test whether the theory can be extended to the subject of interracial people by regressing residential segregation, racial equality, and minority group size on biracial identification incidence among three different racial groups in three separate chapters. To explore what might account for biracial identification incidence differences between racial groups, I reference a totally different body of scholarship: micro-level racial identity work (which is largely qualitative), and micro- and meso-level racial identification work (which is largely quantitative, or both quantitative and qualitative).

Identity is based on one's self-understanding through lived experience (Rockquemore and Brunsma 2008). It is an internalized process perpetually in flux. *Identification*, on the other hand, typically refers to forced-choice classifications on institutional forms (Hirschman, Alba and Farley 2000; Hitlin, Brown and Elder 2006; Saperstein 2006). Empiricists depend on racial identification, rather than racial identity, when research relies on the quantitative analysis of a significant sample size across multiple racial groups and geographies (Brown, Hitlin and Elder 2006; Renn 2008). And that's the case here. I focus on racial identification, but I integrate findings from relevant racial identity studies as appropriate.

One of the most methodologically thorough racial identity pieces I've seen is by Rockquemore and Brunsma (2008). They present several multiracial identity models after examining multi-level independent variables collected through a solid mix of collection modes. The *border identity* is where biracial individuals don't really consider themselves one race or the other, but rather a hybrid with a unique racial classification all its own: "multiracial." This model would argue that Blacks who are half White, for example, would sooner be classified with Asians who are half White than they would with monoracial Blacks (or monoracial Whites for that matter). When asked if they're White or Black, this group would say "neither, I'm mixed," and they fought for (and lost) the right to officially be counted with this designation on the 2000 Census. As a consequence, they select the "Other" box on the census and write in "mixed," "multi," or "multiracial" without writing in any specific racial combination. If they do specify racial categories by checking those boxes or by writing it on the line next to the "Other" box, the Census Bureau recodes them into the racial groups specified (rejecting their attempt to identify with a unique hybrid designation).

In contrast, the *protean identity* is where biracial individuals consider themselves "both." This model would argue that someone who is half Black and half White, for example, would identify with both Blacks and Whites, or fluidly identify with Blacks in some contexts, and with Whites in others. The Black majority fought for (and won) the right for these individuals to officially be counted with more than one racial designation on the 2000 Census, and the "choose all that apply" designation has remained on the 2010 and 2020 questionnaires. These individuals check as many boxes as they desire, and the advantage for the Black majority is they don't lose the headcount they depend on for sociopolitical solidarity.

Then there's the *transcendent identity* model where biracial individuals consider themselves "people" and eschew the very notion of racial designations. These folks would theoretically select the "Other" box on the census and write in "human," "fuck you," or leave the write-in area blank altogether. (See Washington 2017 for congruent thinking applying transgender concepts to transracial contexts.) Without any further details about these respondents, the Census Bureau has no choice but to designate these individuals as "Other."

Finally, there are the *singular identity* models, where a person who is part Black simply identifies as Black alone (per historical social norms) or identifies as White alone (once referred to as *passing*). To be clear, interracial respondents may have identified monoracially on the censuses deployed since 2000, despite having the freedom to identify with more than one race. As such, it's impossible to know just how many people truly are multiracial, but it doesn't really matter. Race is a social construction, and this book is focused on which factors influence the likelihood of identifying with more than one race, regardless of whether increased biracial identification incidence over time is indicative of more biracial people being born, or more biracial people choosing to shift from a singular identity to a protean identity. I argue that either attribution would point toward a reduced social distance between races, and that is what is of interest here. By deploying a macrostructural interracial identification study under a macrostructural interracial marriage framework, and then explaining group differences in the findings using micro- and meso-level racial identity and identification empiricism, I hope to contribute to both demography and race bodies of scholarship.

OUTLINE OF THE BOOK

As I'll explain in chapter 1, Blau's theory depends on the comparison of two groups in which one is a minority group and the other is a majority group. Empirical studies testing the theory within the context of race most consistently choose Whites as the majority group and either Blacks (Blau and Blau 1982; Fitzpatrick and Hwang 1992) or all non-Whites (Blau 1994; Blau et al. 1984; Blau and Schwartz 1984; Blum 1984; South and Messner 1986) as the minority group. More recent tests of Blau's theory investigate other racial groups such as Asians (Heaton and Jacobson 2000; Hwang, Saenz and Aguirre 1994, 1997; Qian 1997, 1999) and Hispanics (Heaton and Jacobson 2000; Qian 1997, 1999), but these are far less common.

Much like empiricism on biracial marriage and other forms of interracial relations, biracial identification empiricism gravitates toward Black and White contexts. Methodological convenience from large sample sizes aside, Blacks and Whites are important groups to study together for many reasons. Blacks differ from other racial groups in their relationship to Whites on factors such as immigration type, timing, and push/pull factors (Castles and Miller 2003), historical oppression and relationship to Whites over time (Wilson 1980), social standing in today's racial hierarchy (Lee and Bean 2004, 2007a, 2007b), and degree of phenotypical dissimilarity with Whites (Townsend et al. 2012). The long and violent history of slavery and racism persistently rears its ugly head in so many aspects of today's contemporary society. Blacks and Whites experience more social, cultural, and spatial distance from one another than any other racial pairing (Massey and Denton 1993; Qian 1999). We see this in the fact that Blacks and Whites are the least likely groups to marry each other (Edmonston, Lee and Passel 2002; Heaton and Jacobson 2000; Qian 1997).

Yet, as I show in the next chapter, biracial Blacks share more heritage with Whites than any other racial group. Nonetheless, Blacks with recent multiracial heritage are the least likely multiracial group to claim multiracial identification (Bratter 2007; Lee and Bean 2007b; Loveman and Muniz 2007). The iconoclasts that do report Black-White biracial identification are therefore of considerable substantive interest, hence the preponderance of quality empiricism analyzing these individuals over the years. And because I seek to determine the degree to which Blau's macrostructural theory of intergroup relations (which is most often tested on Blacks and Whites) can be extended to intergroup identification, I first model Black biracial identification with Whites in chapter 2. Here I hypothesize that Blacks are more likely to biracially identify with Whites when (1) Blacks have greater residential exposure to Whites, (2) educational equality between Blacks and Whites is minimized, and (3) Blacks account for a small proportion of the population relative to Whites.

In chapter 3, I investigate Asian biracial identification with Whites in a model to determine if the theory's explanatory value remains steadfast beyond the realm of Black and White. Here I hypothesize that Asians biracially identify with Whites under similar circumstances as Blacks identify with Whites, but perhaps with softer magnitude.

I then evaluate the relevance of Blau's macrostructural theory to non-White biracial groups, such as Blacks and Asians, in chapter 4. I develop two different models to better understand inter-minority dynamics. I hypothesize that Blacks biracially identify with Asians under similar circumstances as they biracially identify with Whites, but the reverse is not true. Meaning, I don't expect Asians will biracially identify with Blacks under similar circumstances as they biracially identify with Whites. With this dual approach, I contrast the meaning of "minority" as a numerical construct with the idea of "minority" defined by oppression.

As the two largest biracial groups today, Black-Whites and Asian-Whites are of particular interest because they are thought to represent two rather different social standings in the American racial hierarchy. The degree to which the incidence of each of these two groups is dissimilarly explained by macrostructural theory will shed light on the degree to which non-Black minorities are subjected to consequences of *hypodescents*, more commonly known as the *one-drop rule*, a societal phenomenon that commands biracial individuals default to the identity or identification of their minority half (see Davis 1991). To complete the trifecta, however, I also investigate biracial Black-Asians to illuminate inter-minority dynamics often overlooked by a predisposition toward White/non-White groups studied in the literature.

Blau's theory explains the likelihood of intergroup relations and therefore rests on the assumption that there is some degree of social distance between the two groups. Indeed, if the two groups lacked social distance, there would be no sociological phenomenon worth explaining and relationships among members from the two groups would not be noteworthy. As such, the extent to which the theory accounts for two groups coming together arguably alludes to the extent to which the two groups stand apart from one another. Under this line of reasoning, I conclude by asserting that the stronger the explanatory power of each model, the greater the social distance between the two racial groups analyzed in that model.

In the final chapter, I consider what might account for differences between models and what it says about our progress on the racial integration journey in America. As alluded to earlier, there are major differences between Blacks and Asians in immigration timing, patterns, and causes (Castles and Miller 2003), the historical and contemporary relationship to Whites over time (Wilson 1980), today's social standing in the American racial hierarchy (Lee and Bean 2004, 2007a, 2007b), phenotypical similarity or dissimilarity with Whites (Townsend et al. 2012), and therefore patterns and processes of identity selection (Lou, Lalonde and Wilson 2011). The impact of these types of factors on social integration trajectories persists today and continues to affect different racial groups differently.

CONCLUSION

Identifying and measuring the macrostructural dynamics influencing the degree of social distance between two groups is important because it opens the pathway for change. In the context of the 2020 American interracial relations landscape, there is mounting motivation for stark change across the board. The BLM movement has inspired people of all races around the world to show support for the need to change in the United States. Deliberate and drastic change is in order, and the sense of urgency here could not be greater.

To understand some of the structural dynamics contributing to racial distance over the past several decades, interracial marriage has historically been the most common type of interracial phenomena tested by scholars of Blau's macrostructural theory. Contemporary American society, however, is characterized by widespread cohabitation, partnerships not legally recognized as marriage, divorce, and non-marital childbearing. The flexibility of the "check all that apply" race question, new as of the 2000 Census, more accurately tallies variations in racial groups than ever before.

Armed with this type of data, refreshed in 2010, this study hopes to make several contributions to our understanding of race in America. First, it extends Peter Blau's macrostructural theory to an entirely different type of interracial phenomenon. Blau's (1977) theory was on intergroup relations, or *interrelations*. Blau constituents repeatedly tested the theory on intermarriage, especially interracial marriage. This book tests the theory on interracial identification for the first time.

Second, this book seizes the opportunity to take advantage of newly established data to examine the relative suitability of biracial identification as an emerging racial distance indicator. Based on the assumption that people are tangible and marriage is (to some degree) ceremonial, I hypothesize that the relationship between certain structural factors and interracial people will be stronger than the relationship between those same structural factors and interracial marriage. In the same way interracial marriage has reflected racial integration in the past, biracial identification may represent a sharper, more salient indicator of integration in today's society (Kalmijn 1993)—now that large-scale data is available. Armed with large-scale data on biracial *people* in place of data on biracial *marriage*, demographers partnering with social policy makers can make more informed decisions influencing racial integration (Bean and Stevens 2003; Bratter 2007; Lee and Bean 2004). Therefore, I propose substituting interracial marriage with interracial identification as the preferred macrostructural measurement of racial distance.

Third, I analyze other racial pairings, in addition to an emphasis on Black and White. Neither a theoretical extension nor a change in social distance indicators would be appropriate if the connection only applied to Blacks and Whites. Although addressing the race problem between Blacks and Whites is primary—undeniably the first order of business, my hope is that this analytic design will help inform policy protecting any racial group experiencing discrimination, hate crimes, and everything in between. Importantly, my multiple racial pairing design provides a relative point of comparison to the Black-White test for determining whether there is evidence of a multi-tiered racial hierarchy, as opposed to a dichotomous social structure (i.e., White/non-White or Black/non-Black) as some scholars suggest.

Fourth, I attempt to fill a gap in the literature by replicating a single analytic design on multiple racial groups so that apples-to-apples comparisons can be made across racial groups. How different groups are impacted by macrostructural variables differently is critical. Importantly, this design will help me to quantitatively estimate the approximate placement of each racial group on a multi-tiered racial hierarchy. It may be common knowledge among academic sociologists that Whites are at the top, Blacks are at the bottom, and Asians are somewhere in between. But are Asians equidistant between Whites and Blacks? Or closer to one anchor or the other? Quantifying the relativity between groups helps us to truly understand just how far the group on the bottom will need to be brought up to create an equitable society.

The fifth contribution of this book is that it presents a better understanding of inter-minority dynamics. I complete a trifecta between Blacks, Whites, and Asians by examining double-minority models including both Asians and Blacks (without Whites). It's the first analysis of its kind to examine the applicability of Blau's theory of intergroup relations to two specified non-White racial groups in the United States with statistically significant results, and it also fills a gap in the racial identification literature. By comparing the percentage of Asians identifying as half[4] Black to the percentage of Blacks identifying as half Asian, and then comparing these models to the Black-White and Asian-White models, I'm able to uniquely paint a clear picture of racial distance between groups from each minority group's perspective. The double-minority models also allow me to deconstruct the meaning of "minority" by contrasting the meaning as numerical with the idea of "minority" defined by prolonged oppression.

The sixth contribution of this book is that it presents a methodological extension of our understanding of racial identification by folding in a fully macro-level perspective. Racial identification has been extensively examined at the micro- and meso-levels. Although it changes over time and context, sociologists have a fairly solid understanding of how personal factors and immediate social contexts influence racial identification. Different race-gender combinations between parents, levels of education, skin tones, personal interactions, experiences, memories, and various sociopsychological factors can impact whether an individual chooses to identify biracially. Religion, politics, news, art, and social movements also play a role, through culture and social tones. But at an even more systemic level are dynamics like residential segregation, wage gaps, inequality in educational attainment, and other macro-level forces happening at the geography-level unit of analysis. These environmental factors are known to influence other interracial behaviors like marriage, friendship, and crime, but might they also influence interracial identification? This book is the first of its kind to answer that question.

NOTES

1. I use the terms *people* and *individuals* throughout the book to reference the social phenomenon under investigation (a person/individual makes the choice on whether to identify with more than one racial category on the census). This reference to people/individuals is meant to be a simple way of distinguishing this study from nearly all comparable studies in the macrostructural field, which focus on *relationships* (between two persons), especially *marriage*. However, people/individuals are neither the dependent variable nor the unit of analysis in this study. Rather, biracial

identification incidences (at group-levels) act as dependent variables, and metropolitan areas act as units of analysis.

2. The intergroup relations theory has been used to explain the probability of several different types of interracial relations, including interracial contact, conflict, and marriage. Marriage has always been the most popular among these.

3. Intermarriage between races is also referred to as *interracial marriage, biracial marriage, mixed-race marriage,* and *exogamy*. I use these terms interchangeably.

4. I use the term *half* throughout the book to simplify descriptions of biracial populations in an effort to reduce overall wordiness and improve readability. Selecting two racial category boxes does not necessarily indicate that an individual is half one and half the other (nor does it necessarily imply that the individual doesn't share heritage with a third racial group). That is, individuals who indicate two races on the census may or may not be composed of 50 percent DNA of one group and 50 percent of the other. More likely, individuals who are aware of any degree of partial mixed heritage and who wish for that partial heritage to be reflected on the census will check the additional box indicating that heritage. The proportionate mix of heritage is outside of the scope of this manuscript.

Chapter 1

Structural Influence

This book assesses the effects of macrostructural variables on the likelihood of White, Black, and Asian Americans reporting biracial identification with one another on the 2010 U.S. Census. I evaluate the extent social forces known to influence interracial marriage also influence interracial identification by testing whether macrostructural theory can be extended beyond explaining the likelihood two different-race people will have relations (i.e., marry), to the likelihood one person will identify with two different races. Macrostructural theory (Blau 1977, 1994) asserts three key factors as influencing the likelihood of interracial phenomena. First, the number of characteristics in common affects the likelihood of meaningful exposure between members of two different races. Second, equality affects the availability of same-race, same-status relationship options. A third element, group size, plays a role within each of these two key factors.

Similar to prior macrostructural theory research, I operationalize these factors using residential segregation, racial equality, and minority group size, respectively, for each of 363 metropolitan areas in the continental United States. I then regress these factors onto Black-White, Asian-White, and Black-Asian incidence in three separate chapters. I use data from the 2010 U.S. Census, which allowed respondents the freedom to choose multiple racial categories to identify one's self. A preliminary study of similar inquiry and structure was conducted using data from the prior decennial census (Butts 2008). Minor research design revisions were implemented in the current study as presented here.

EXTENDING THE THEORETICAL FRAMEWORK
OF INTERGROUP RELATIONS

Intergroup phenomena are often investigated through the lens of exchange (Blau 1964; Homans 1958), assimilation (Gordon 1964; Park 1926), or opportunity-structure (Blau 1977, 1994; Simmel 1908) perspectives. Both exchange theory and assimilation theory have been criticized as being Anglo-conformist and over-reliant on economic motivations (Bean and Stevens 2003; Blau 1994). That is, both would only be able to explain why a Black person would identify as also White, but not why a White person would identify as also Black or why a Black person would identify as also Asian, for example.

Opportunity-structure theory, on the other hand, examines the distribution of a multitude of social positions (Blau 1977), thereby welcoming any group defined by any type of demographic categorization of sufficient sample size into the analysis. Furthermore, the opportunity-structure approach has the macro-level ability of examining the environmental constraints within which intergroup social processes are permitted. These constraints are believed to wield a greater degree of influence on social life than micro- and meso-level approaches (Blau 1977). Therefore, the effect of macrostructural forces on the likelihood of meaningful social interaction between members of different groups is examined through the opportunity-structure perspective.

This perspective rests on Simmel's (1908) notion of *over-lapping social circles* where each social circle is based on a demographic or lifestyle characteristic. The characteristic that is most salient is the social circle in which the person feels the most belonging. This becomes their core identity group, or in a sense, an internal kind of master status. People generally prefer to interact with members of their own group. However, Simmel argues that meaningful social relationships can happen between people from different groups if they are similar in many other ways (i.e., if their other social circles intersect substantially). These commonalities become the grounds on which social relationships can be formed despite belonging to different core groups.

Peter Blau (1977, 1994) operationalized the opportunity-structure perspective with his *macrostructural theory of intergroup relations*. Blau agreed with Simmel that people prefer relationships with members of their own group but do sometimes have relationships with members outside their group when there is enough in common. Where Blau added to Simmel's work was in his conjecture that the likelihood of this happening is facilitated by certain environmental factors in the macrostructure. That is, certain macrostructural parameters can hinder opportunities to fulfill in-group relationship preferences, while other parameters present opportunities that facilitate relationships outside the group. Examples of these parameters include *demographic consolidation* (i.e., the extent group membership is correlated with several other demographic and lifestyle characteristics at once, resulting in different groups having very little exposure to one another and very little in common at that), *equality* between groups, and *relative group size*.

An examination of this process depends on the comparison of groups unevenly distributed across a social hierarchy of some kind. The theory lends itself to "race" as the demographic characteristic defining group membership. The interracial phenomena examined through this lens by scholars in the past include interracial contact, conflict, friendship, and most often marriage. Interracial marriage has been cited by many scholars as a social distance indicator between racial groups. While interracial identification has also been regarded by scholars as a racial distance measure, published empiricism has not yet tested the extent to which macrostructural theory can be extended beyond explaining the likelihood persons from two different races will have relations or marry, to the likelihood persons in one group will identify with two different races.

This book examines whether the same social forces known to influence interracial relations, and interracial marriage in particular, also influence interracial identification. Therefore, the central research question is: Do macrostructural forces known to influence biracial marriage also influence biracial identification? Identifying and measuring the macrostructural dynamics influencing the likelihood of biracial identification over monoracial identification is important because it may shed light on the degree of social distance between two groups in a new way and therefore has the potential to open the pathway for change.

Interracial marriage, a respected racial integration metric, has by far been the most common type of interracial phenomena tested under Blau's macrostructural theory over the past several decades. Contemporary American society, however, is characterized by widespread cohabitation, partnerships not legally recognized as marriage, divorce, and non-marital childbearing. The flexibility of the "check all that apply" race question, new as of the 2000 Census, more accurately tallies variations in racial groups than ever before. This gives demographers the opportunity to utilize data on biracial *people*, rather than biracial *marriage*, as an emerging social distance indicator (Bean and Stevens 2003; Bratter 2007; Lee and Bean 2004). In the same way interracial marriage has reflected racial integration in the past, biracial identification may represent a more salient indicator of racial integration today (Kalmijn 1993).

GENERAL RESEARCH DESIGN

The goal of this section is to explain the details of the analytic design. This is necessary for several reasons. Namely, this is the first study of its kind. It would be my hope that other scholars would find reasons and ways to repeat the analysis, and ideally improve upon it. Secondly, this book repurposes and therefore re-operationalizes an existing theory. As such, part of its contribution to the literature is methodological in nature.

To test whether macrostructural forces known to influence other interracial phenomena influence interracial identification, this study examines cities, rather than individuals. MSAs are compared on the basis of White, Black, and Asian biracial identification incidence. Such a comparison requires a quantitative approach. The ultimate source of racial identification incidence aggregated at the city level in the United States is the Census. Both the 2000 Census and the 2010 Census allowed respondents to self-identify with as many racial categories as desired. The pilot for this study utilized the 2000 Census, while this study utilizes the 2010 Census. The decennial census also provides aggregated racial data for two of the three primary independent variables and one of the two control variables incorporated into this analysis. Variables not available through the decennial census are available from the Census Bureau's ACS. Additional details with rationale for this design are described here.

Unit of Analysis

Social structure is embodied by multidimensional social arrangements between groups within proximity of one another. "Population structures and their effects on rates of social relations . . . must be based on a sample of populations, not of individuals" (Blau 1994:53). In the United States, urban centers are characterized by diverse populations living in close proximity (McPherson, Smith-Lovin and Cook 2001). Metropolitan areas have been the primary pallet for examining interracial contact since the antebellum period (Wilson 1980). MSAs are defined by the census as urban centers with at least 50,000 residents (U.S. Office of Management and Budget 2013). Metropolitan areas present natural units of analysis for comparing geographical differences in macrostructural forces and biracial identification incidence.

Analysis Type

The emphasis on a macro-level unit of analysis in this book directly affects the analysis type. A *qualitative* approach has the advantage of explaining how individuals make sense of their personal and social environments and internalize interpretations (Glesne 2006). Qualitative research consists of collecting information to understand phenomena that are not generally quantifiable, such as experiences and interpretations. As such, qualitative research tends to focus on the individual (rather than the environment) as the unit of analysis. Collection methods include interpersonal settings with interviews, focus groups, and so on. Most prior research on biracial subjects utilizes this approach for these reasons (see Chideya 1999; Root 1992; Waters 1999; Wright et al. 2003; Zack 1995).

A *quantitative* approach on the other hand consists of collecting information that can be measured numerically. It is used to find patterns and trends, statistically test the relationship between numerically measurable things, and so on. Importantly, quantitative research tends to capture larger sample sizes (often through self-reported surveys), making conclusions drawn from it more suitable for making inferences about the broader population than qualitative research. Quantitative methods are necessary for the analysis of large-scale social structures and processes, such as those that may influence interracial identification. The comparison of racial identification incidence across metropolitan areas requires a quantitative approach. Therefore, quantitative analysis is utilized in this study of biracial identification incidence.

DATA SOURCES

The 2010 Census reports on 363 continental U.S. metropolitan areas,[1] all of which are used. Racial identification and most of the explanatory macrostructural phenomena expected to vary with racial identification incidence are available from the 2010 Census. Others are available from pooled, five-year estimates of the ACS.

Census

The ultimate source of racial identification counts in the United States is the decennial census. Because the census comprehensively counts the total U.S. population, it provides greater sample size than any other source of racial identification.

There are some concerns about census data. First, Brunsma (2006) argues that the census should not be used for studies on biracial people because it reflects social and cultural discourse. That is, biracial identification incidence may wax and wane as macrosocial tones fluctuate. However, this very reasoning ironically supports using census data for my analysis *because* structural variables encompass social and cultural discourse so well. Second, Harris and Sim (2002) argue the census does not count the biracial population, it counts *a* biracial population. However, this very phenomenon is precisely what is under investigation: if actual biracial identification incidence across metropolitan areas is greater than reported biracial identification incidence, then there is a predisposition toward monoracial identification, and this has meaning. Indeed, the ratio of Blacks to Whites, for example, is 0.182, yet the percentage of Blacks identifying as biracial with Whites is only 4.4 percent—a mere quarter of what would be expected due to chance. This indicates that there is a predisposition toward monoracial identification among Blacks. Therefore, the social conditions under which iconoclasts do choose biracial identification over the monoracial default are of considerable substantive interest. And the degree to which different racial minority groups exercise this option may speak to different degrees of social distance between different racial groups.

Method

Since 1790, the U.S. Census Bureau counts the entire population once a decade. Each household receives a letter in March of the census year preparing recipients for the questionnaire (U.S. Census Bureau 2010). Heads of households are asked to complete a single survey on behalf of their entire household as of April 1. Prior to 2020, the census questionnaire was in most cases delivered and returned by mail. Today a survey link with a log-on code is available for households with access to the internet. Whether completed online or on paper, one thing is for certain—completion is required by the constitution for every person residing in the United States on a given date.

At the end of April 2010, 28 percent of households had yet to respond. This is typical, as the figure was exactly the same at the end of April 2000 (Justis 2010). Census Bureau representatives follow up on these non-responsive households in May. Completed questionnaires are returned to processing offices where responses are digitally recorded. In 2010, nearly 309 million persons were counted. The data is rigorously cleansed. Missing data and problematic or questionable responses to individual questions are handled by directly contacting the household for clarification. Data is then aggregated for all areas and reported to governmental leaders by December 31 of the census year.[2]

Participants

The U.S. Constitution requires that every single person in America be counted, regardless of citizenship status. The person completing the questionnaire is asked to count and briefly describe every single person of any age who lives or sleeps in the household most of the time. Family members in college, prison, nursing home, military, and so forth are not to be counted by the permanent address respondent because they will be counted on the questionnaire delivered to their temporary address as of April 1. Respondents are however asked to count and describe anyone temporarily staying at the address on April 1 if they lack a permanent address.

Householders are assured that information gathered by the census will remain confidential by law. That is, individual responses provided to the Census Bureau cannot be used for any purpose other than for counting the population and summarizing population counts by sex, age, ethnicity, and race. Furthermore, data on each person must be aggregated enough such that specific individuals cannot be identified in published data files or reports.

Instrument

After reading the instructions described earlier, 2010 Census respondents were asked how many people stayed at the address on April 1, 2010. For validity, respondents were then asked if additional people (e.g., children, relatives, non-relatives, or transients) not indicated in the response to the first question, stayed at the dwelling place on April 1. Next the respondent was asked if the dwelling is owned, rented, or neither, and then the phone number where the respondent could be reached in the event that certain responses required clarity.

Respondents were then asked to describe each person counted in the first question sequentially. Descriptions include last name, first name, gender, age on April 1, and birthday for validity. Instructions precede the next section: "NOTE: Please answer BOTH Question 8 about Hispanic origin and Question 9 about race. For this census, Hispanic origins are not races." Question 8 asked whether the person being described is of Hispanic, Latino, or Spanish origin. Question 9 asked the respondent to describe the race of that same person. (The details of this key question will be explained further below.) Finally, for validity, respondents were asked whether the person being described was staying somewhere else on April 1 (such as at college, in prison, at a nursing home, or in military quarters). The respondent completed this battery for up to six people. If seven or more people resided in the household on April 1, only their name, sex, age, and whether they are related to person 1 were asked. Census Bureau representatives may have followed up to inquire about Hispanic ethnicity and race of these individuals afterward.

American Community Survey

The instrument described earlier was referred to as the *short form* until the 2010 Census. In prior censuses, one in every six households received a much longer form. This form, referred to as the *long form*, asked the same questions as the short form with the addition of many more. This included questions on topics such as work commute, income, education, housing, citizenship, ancestry, and language spoken at home. With the 2010 Census, however, every household received the short form. Data on topics from what had been the long form are now collected through the ACS.

The ACS was developed to allow the census to focus on its fundamental priority: to count the population (U.S. Census Bureau 2010). The ACS has two advantages over the prior census long form (U.S. Census Bureau 2009). First, demographic data is collected on an ongoing basis. More current data means analyses are also more current and therefore are more relevant. Additionally, continuously collected data are arguably more sensitive to the detection of change and trends. Second, more detailed information about people living in sparse geographic areas can be released without violating confidentially because time periods can be pooled such that specific individuals cannot be identified. ACS findings are published annually using rolling data aggregated at one-year, three-year, and five-year levels, depending on the granularity necessary to maintain confidentiality.[3]

Although general metropolitan area-level data is often releasable in single-year increments, slicing the data by demographic characteristics, such as by race and education, or race and nativity (as in the current study), makes data on some metropolitan areas not releasable in increments of less than five years. The ACS data used in this study is based on pooled, five-year estimates for data collected from 2007 to 2011. These data became available in 2012 at the same time 2010 Census data was published and the data file for this study was compiled.

Method

Nearly 300,000 addresses are randomly selected each month from the Master Address File (MAF) of over 180 million residences in the United States, giving each a 1-in-480 chance of selection in a given month (U.S. Census Bureau 2013). The ACS is completed by at least 175,000 households and persons in group quarters each month, all year long, every year. Each household receives a notification letter through the U.S. Postal Service. Soon afterward, instructions for completing the survey online are mailed. Non-responsive households are then mailed a reminder postcard, followed by a paper questionnaire. Remaining non-responsive households are sent a second reminder postcard before they are contacted by telephone. A random sample of persistent non-responsive households are then visited by a Census Bureau representative. Completed questionnaires are returned to processing offices where responses are digitally recorded. The data is rigorously cleansed. Missing data and problematic or questionable responses to individual questions are handled by directly contacting the household for clarification. Data are then aggregated to varying geographic granularities.

Participants

Similar to the census, a single person at the residence completes a single survey on the behalf of all individuals in the household. The person completing the questionnaire is asked to describe in detail the dwelling and every single person of any age living or staying at the address for at least two months, as well as any individuals staying at the address less than two months if they have no other residence. Family members away in college, prison, nursing homes, military barracks, and so on for at least two months are not to be described by the respondent at the permanent address.

Instrument

The 2007–2011 ACS gathered data on personal and housing characteristics, rather than just population counts. Demographic, social, economic, and housing topics were covered. After reading the instructions described earlier, respondents were asked to indicate the current date, their name, phone number, and the number of people staying at the address. Respondents were then asked to describe each person counted in the previous question sequentially. Descriptions included last name, first name, relation to respondent, gender, age, and birthday for validity. Instructions preceded the next section: "NOTE: Please answer BOTH Question 5 about Hispanic origin and Question 6 about race. Hispanic origins are not races." Question 5 asked whether the person being described is of Hispanic, Latino, or Spanish origin. Question 6 asked the respondent to describe the race of the person being described.

After the next section covering housing characteristics, the respondent returned to describing each person in the household in further detail beginning with nativity, citizenship, and migration year, and proceeding with details on education. The next questions covered ancestry, language spoken at home, English proficiency, prior residence, health insurance coverage, health, marital history, kin, military involvement, employment, and commuting for work and income. The respondent completed this battery for each person in the household.

For data collected from 2007 to 2011, completed sample size, coverage rates, response rates, and allocation rates for questions utilized in this study are as follows (U.S. Census Bureau 2013). Nearly 10.6 million surveys were completed between 2007 and 2011. The response rate was above 97 percent every year, indicating strong data quality. Household coverage rates exceeded 98 percent and group quarters coverage rates exceeded 79 percent. The latter indicates that people living in group quarters such as those in college, prison, nursing homes, or military barracks have about a 20 percent chance of not being selected to complete the survey when they should have been. Because this error is associated with bias, ACS estimates are adjusted to align with independent population controls (i.e., sex, age, race, and Hispanic ethnicity) produced by the decennial census. Allocation rates will be discussed here.

HYPOTHESIZING THE INFLUENCE OF STRUCTURE ON BIRACIAL IDENTIFICATION

The data sources described provide data that fit nicely with Peter Blau's macrostructural theory. Blau lays out the way his theory should be tested in a straightforward way (Blau and Schwartz 1984; Blau 1994). The dependent variable is the prevalence of metropolitan area residents exercising intergroup relations. The most important independent variable is the degree to which groups are socially, culturally, and geographically isolated from one another (i.e., "consolidation" or its inverse, "intersection"). A second independent variable measures group differences in distribution across social positions on a status-oriented demographic dimension, such as income or education (i.e., inequality). A third independent variable plays a role in the first two and therefore must be controlled (i.e., relative group size). But because the effect of group size is substantively interesting on its own standing, it is not categorized in this analysis with other control variables, such as foreign-born population incidence (sometimes referred to as *nativity incidence* in this manuscript) and geographic region.

The central research question asks whether structural factors theorized to affect intergroup relationships and empirically shown to influence biracial marriage also influence biracial identification. Hence,

H_1. The more social circles between members of two different races intersect, the greater the likelihood racial minorities will report biracial identification with the majority group.

H_2. The greater the educational equality between two racial groups, the greater the likelihood racial minorities will report monoracial identification.

H_3. The smaller the racial minority group size relative to the racial majority group size, the greater the likelihood racial minorities will report biracial identification with the majority group.

ANALYSIS TECHNIQUE

Because macrostructural forces are inherently correlated, the effects of each independent variable must be isolated with multiple regression. To test the simultaneous effect of demographic consolidation (i.e., exposure), educational inequality, relative group size, nativity incidence, and geographic region on the likelihood of biracial identification on the census, Ordinary Least Squares (OLS) regression is performed. Four separate regressions are presented in the following chapters. In the first analysis (chapter 2), the effect of Black segregation, educational inequality between Blacks and Whites, Black group size relative to Whites, the percentage of the Black population foreign-born, and geographic region of each metropolitan area is regressed on Black-White biracial identification incidence in each metropolitan area. In the second analysis (chapter 3), the effect of Asian segregation, educational inequality between Asians and Whites, Asian group size relative to Whites, the percentage of the Asian population foreign-born, and geographic region of each metropolitan area is regressed on Asian-White biracial identification incidence in each metropolitan area. In chapter 4, the same macrostructural parameters are examined to test their impact on the likelihood Blacks identify as half Asian, and then again on the likelihood Asians identify as half Black. This chapter includes two regression models in order to be able to position each of these two racial groups as the minority in the model.

Multiple regression analysis is a statistical technique estimating the relationship between several independent variables and a single dependent variable. Multiple regression analysis was developed as a way to estimate the relative importance of multiple independent variables simultaneously in predicting a given independent variable (Knoke, Bohrnstedt and Mee 2002). OLS regression estimates the relative importance of each independent variable in a way that minimizes the sum of squared residuals (Wooldridge 2006).

Regression is arguably the most commonly used statistical technique in social research (Fox 1991). One advantage lies in its versatility. It can be used in econometric analysis, consumer behavior research, program evaluation, feasibility studies, and of course traditional social research such as in this study (Hair et al. 2006). Another advantage is that it allows for the explicit control of any number of factors, which is often necessary when using non-experimental data (Wooldridge 2006). Furthermore, multiple regression can accommodate any number of independent variables (within reason). This not only allows for more comprehensive explanatory power than other techniques, but also allows for some degree of causal inference (Wooldridge 2006).

The earliest conceptualization of multiple regression is traced back to Sir Francis Galton (Ellis 1994). A cousin of Charles Darwin, Galton's seminal work in this area arose out of his study on sweet peas. By finding himself in need of a way to simultaneously evaluate the independent contributions of multiple genetic sources on a given pea's characteristics, he laid the groundwork for what would become modern regression—by implementing a multivariate experimental design planting seeds, plotting the resulting data, and discovering the regression line (Stanton 2001).

The regression equation is written as:

$$Y = \alpha + \beta_1(X_1) + \beta_2(X_2) + \beta_3(X_3) + \beta_4(X_4) + \beta_5(X_5)$$

where Y is the dependent variable, X is each independent variable, α is the value of the dependent variable when all independent variables are equal to zero (the intercept), and β indicates the regression coefficient associated with each independent variable. The equation represents the line best representing the relationship between Y and the simultaneous, independent effects of the Xs.

As mentioned, OLS regression estimates the relative importance of each independent variable in a way that minimizes the sum of squared residuals (Wooldridge 2006). The sum of squared residuals can be derived by comparing values of Y observed in the data, to predicted values of Y predicted by the regression equation. Logically, the difference between the two indicates how well the model fits each data point. The difference between the observed and predicted value of each data point is squared to eliminate negative values. Then the squared deviation of all data points is summed. This sum of squared residuals is an indicator of overall model fit. With lower values indicating better model fit, a perfect model has a sum of squared residuals equal to 0, indicating no difference between actual and predicted values of the dependent variable (Hutcheson 2011). With these technical underpinnings in mind, OLS regression coefficients are solved using a series of linear equations that set derivatives to 0 for each record in the sample (Wooldridge 2006). This computation is arduous with even the smallest of sample sizes. Fortunately, statistical software can solve for β by minimizing the sum of squared residuals in an instant. The regression models are calculated in this study using IBM SPSS Professional 23.0.

The regression coefficient of each independent variable is described as: the change in the dependent variable that is associated with a one-unit change in that independent variable (while holding all other independent variables in the model constant). This statistic is useful for explaining the impact of each independent variable on the dependent variable but cannot be easily used to compare the effects of independent variables to each other. When independent variables are measured on different scales, as in this study, *standardized* regression coefficients are useful for determining the relative impact each independent variable has on the dependent variable. In this study, the statistical significance of the effect of each independent variable on the dependent variable is reported at the 0.01 level, unless otherwise noted. This indicates that one can be 99 percent sure that a given statistic is true.

The model as a whole is also evaluated for statistical significance. Both model fit and explanatory power describe the model. As explained, the sum of squares is an indicator of model fit. As the sum of squared residuals decreases, the explanatory power of the model, R^2, increases. R^2 is the percentage of variation in Y explained by the Xs in the model. Higher R^2 indicates greater explanatory power. But because R^2 always increases with each additional X added to the model, *adjusted* R^2 is recommended over R^2 to indicate model explanatory power because it does not automatically increase with each additional X (Hutcheson 2011).

Outliers can be problematic in OLS regression (Fox 1991). One type of outlier is defined as an extreme value relative to most other values of a variable (i.e., values falling outside 3 standard deviations of the mean). This type of outlier can disproportionately sway OLS results. Another type of outlier is defined as a record with an unusual dependent variable, given the independent variables. Whereas identifying either type of outlier is fairly clear-cut, deciding what to do about them is not. Fox (2002) recommends taking note of outliers and investigating why they are unusual, but generally advises against removing them from the analysis because doing so presents a departure from reality. In this analysis, outliers are identified and discussed.

Having too many explanatory variables in an OLS model is also problematic. Although it would seem that the more explanatory variables, the better the model, over-specification limits the degree to which the data can vary, thereby restraining the model equation. Wooldridge (2006) recommends only including explanatory variables theorized or previously proven to affect the dependent variable in the model. Fortunately, a careful study of macrostructural theory and its revisions provides a straightforward guide on which variables to include (Blau 1977, 1994). A pilot study, which will be described in more detail shortly, tested the full range of explanatory variables theorized to affect interracial relations. However, it was concluded that a more parsimonious model was empirically advantageous, and a closer fit to the spirit of the theoretical underpinnings. Therefore, the present study reduces explanatory variables (including controls) from eight to five without losing substantial explanatory power.

Dependence among explanatory variables can also cause problems with OLS by leading to poor predictions (Fox 1991). When some of the independent variables are strongly correlated with one another, it creates a condition in which there are several potential solutions, rather than a single, best-fitting line. Some degree of multicollinearity is inherent among structural variables (Blau 1994). However, multicollinearity statistics performed on these data indicate that thresholds are not violated (see appendix B).

Occasionally, quantitative studies of metropolitan areas utilize multi-level analyses. However, Blau (1994) insists this is unnecessary because the variable capturing overlapping social circles (i.e., demographic consolidation) is itself equivalent to multi-level differentiation. "The theorem of multiple intersection's influence on intergroup relations is the very core of macrostructural opportunity theory" (Blau 1994:69). This macrostructural force, Blau argues, already captures ramifications penetrating multiple ecological levels, thereby eliminating the need to use hierarchical linear modeling (HLM) here.

As mentioned, a plurality of empiricism testing Blau's macrostructural theory examines incidence of interracial marriage as the dependent variable. This is in part due to methodological convenience; marriage was the only type of relation in which the census collected data on both members (Blau 1994). These tests analyzed the number of young couples that intermarry across metropolitan areas. Because differences in the case base inherent in intermarriage incidence violate OLS's assumption of homoscedasticity, these studies most often used weighted least squares (WLS) regression to correct heteroscedasticity (e.g., see Blau and Schwartz 1984; Blau et al. 1984; Blau 1994). With the exception of the pilot study preceding this analysis (discussed at the end of this chapter), this book marks the first time Blau's theory is used to investigate interracial identification.[4] Because the dependent variable in this study is based on interracial identification among individuals, rather than interracial marriage between individuals, the assumption of homoscedasticity is not violated.

Occasionally, quantitative studies of intergroup relations utilize techniques associated with a social network approach. Whereas macrostructure includes incidence of intergroup relations between members of various groups, microstructure includes a network of social ties between the individuals within a group. Giddens (1986) and Coleman (1990) recommend complementing any analysis of macrostructural influence on intergroup relations with an analysis of how the actor/network influences this social structure. However, Blau (1994) responds to these critiques of his theory by insisting his conceptualization of population structure is not produced by the deliberate actions of present-day individuals, thereby dismissing the necessity of incorporating social network-level tests here.

The majority of research on biracial identity is qualitative in nature, examining individuals on a personal level (see Chideya 1999; Root 1992; Waters 1999; Wright et al. 2003; Zack 1995). This is in contrast to the majority of research on biracial identification which is quantitative—by nature of identification being an act in which formal categorization is sought. Although biracial identification studies are taken at the micro-level, meso-level, or both, studies focused on characteristics unique to the individual often make good use of exploratory factor analysis (EFA) or confirmatory factor analysis (CFA) (Cortes et al. 2003). Because the quantitative study described in this book is conducted at the macro-level, examining characteristics of cities, rather than individuals, EFA and CFA are not appropriate here.

This research devises four separate OLS regression models presented in three chapters. Each model can be written as:

Proportion of Race A Claiming Biracial Identification with Race B in Each Metropolitan Area $=$ $\alpha + \beta_{ex}$(Exposure of Race A to Race B) $+ \beta_{eq}$(Equality Between Race A and Race B) $+ \beta_{gs}$(Group Size of Race A Relative to Race B) $+ \beta_{fb}$(Proportion of Race A Foreign Born) $+ \beta_{gr}$(Geographic Region Dummy Variable)

where α is the value of the dependent variable when all independent variables are equal to zero (the intercept), and β indicates the regression coefficient associated with each independent variable. This equation represents the line best representing the relationship between the percentage of a racial minority group claiming biracial identification (i.e., *biracial identification incidence*) and the simultaneous, independent effects of exposure, equality, group size, nativity, and geography.

PILOT STUDY

A preliminary study of similar inquiry and structure was conducted using data from the 2000 Census (Butts 2008). With full-population biracial identification incidence available for the first time in U.S. history, macrostructural parameters across 330 metropolitan areas were examined to evaluate whether social forces historically shown to influence Black-White marriage incidence also influence Black-White biracial identification incidence among Blacks. This study concluded that Black exposure to Whites (segregation), racial inequality (in higher education), Black group size relative to Whites, percent of Blacks foreign-born and geographic region affects the likelihood Blacks report Black-White biracial identification ($R^2 = 93.3$ percent).

The analyses in this book feature a slightly refined approach to operationalizing theoretical constructs, reducing the total number of independent variables from eight to five, and replacing 2000 Census data with that of 2010.

NOTES

1. Metropolitan areas in Hawaii, Alaska, and Puerto Rico were removed because the nature of their geographical confinement and isolation arguably interferes with the structural forces expected to affect interracial identification.

2. Year 2020 was a challenging one for the census. The global COVID-19 pandemic kept U.S. Census workers from tallying many difficult-to reach non-responders. Urban, indigent populations are especially difficult to reach. These populations over-index on people of color, the homeless, and undocumented immigrants. Although the 2020 timeline was initially adjusted to allow time to reach these populations after "shelter-in-place" orders were lifted later that same year, the Supreme Court agreed

to the Trump administration's election-year request to close the books on the decennial population count *before the entire population was counted.* It is unclear at the time of this writing the severity of the undercount (Liptak and Wines 2020). Scholars interested in repeating this study using 2020 data will need to take these factors into account.

3. Data on areas or groups of more than 65,000 people are available in single-year increments because it would be impossible to identify specific individuals. Areas or groups of less than 20,000 people are aggregated at the five-year level. Data on areas or groups of 20,000 to 64,999 people are aggregated at the three-year level.

4. Other quantitative studies of biracial identification (which do not employ macrostructural theory) utilize logit or multinomial logit models. However, the unit of analysis in those studies is at the individual level, not the metropolitan area level. That is, independent variables describe the actual people identifying as biracial, which is not the case here.

Chapter 2

Structural Influence on Black Biracial Identification with Whites

The 2000 U.S. Census allowed respondents to describe themselves with more than one racial for the first time in history. Approximately 6.8 million chose this option. This figure grew more than three times the total American population growth rate by the 2010 Census. Among 42 million Blacks (13.6 percent of the American population), nearly 2.7 million identified as biracial (see table 2.1). Over 1.8 million, or 4.4 percent of the total Black population, specifically identified as also White. Although doubled from 2.2 percent in 2000, this is much smaller than what would be expected due to chance, given the ratio of Blacks to Whites is 0.18. Responses to the census race question confirm that racial identification is indeed a choice (Harris and Sim 2002; Hirschman 2004; Masuoka 2011). Now the question becomes which factors influence that choice and why.

One factor influencing the racial identification choice is ironically overlooked: racial identity (Brunsma 2006). Identity is based on one's self-understanding through lived experience (Rockquemore and Brunsma 2008). Because it is an internalized process perpetually in flux, it often does not, or cannot, match forced-choice classifications on institutional forms (Hirschman, Alba and Farley 2000; Hitlin, Brown and Elder 2006; Rockquemore and Brunsma 2008; Saperstein 2006). Nonetheless, empiricists depend on racial identification, rather than racial identity, when research relies on the quantitative analysis of a significant sample size across multiple racial groups and geographies (Brown, Hitlin and Elder 2006; Renn 2008).

There is considerable geographic variation in the percentage of Blacks identifying as biracial with Whites. In the 2010 Census for example, as few as 0.6 percent of Blacks in Jackson, Mississippi, identified as also White, while as many as 42.2 percent of Blacks in Coeur d'Alene, Idaho identified as also White. It seems that greater biracial populations tend to skew toward areas

Table 2.1   **Racial Identification Frequencies in the United States**

Description of Racial Categories Selected	Count of People	Percent of Total Population
One Race (Total)	299,736,465	97.08%
White	223,553,265	72.41%
Black or African American	38,929,319	12.61%
Asian	14,674,252	4.75%
American Indian and Alaska Native	2,932,248	0.95%
Native Hawaiian and Other Pacific Islander	540,013	0.17%
Other Race	19,107,368	6.19%
Two Races (Total)	8,265,318	2.68%
White; Black or African American	1,834,212	0.59%
White; Asian	1,623,234	0.53%
White; Other Racial Groups	3,343,224	1.08%
Black or African American; Asian	185,595	0.06%
Black or African American; Other Groups	634,300	0.21%
Asian; Other Racial Groups	458,981	0.15%
Other Biracial Groups	185,772	0.06%
Three+ Races	743,755	0.24%
Total Population	308,745,538	100.00%

Source: Summary File 1 (SF1), Prefixed Table 8 (P8), Census (2010), U.S. Census Bureau.

where Blacks represent a relatively small proportion of the population (Butts 2008). Distinctions like these across metropolitan areas hint of underlying structural differences affecting the likelihood of Black biracial identification with Whites. Borrowing from prior theoretical and empirical scholarship on mixed-race marriage, I explore how urban structural factors affecting intergroup relations between Blacks and Whites impact the likelihood Black Americans report mixed-race identification with Whites.

STRUCTURAL FACTORS AFFECTING BLACK RELATIONSHIPS WITH WHITES

Intergroup relations are often investigated through the lens of exchange, assimilation, or opportunity-structure perspectives. Peter Blau's macro-structural theory develops the opportunity-structure perspective (Blau 1977, 1994). This perspective rests on Simmel's (1908) notion of over-lapping social circles where each social circle is based on a demographic (or lifestyle) characteristic. The demographic characteristic that is most salient is the social circle in which the person feels the most belonging. This is their core identity group, though this may be moderately situational. Under some circumstances, one's gender dominates one's core identity and presides over what is considered in-group versus out-group. Choice of sports teams or shopping companions might be an example. In other situations, one's age bracket is the determining factor, such as when choosing another couple to vacation with or to invite to a house party. Friendships tend to be a bit more flexible when it comes to race. But when it comes to marriage, marrying within one's racial group is still the dominant social norm. (This is not surprising since interracial marriage wasn't legal in all fifty states until just a few decades ago!)

Regardless of which demographic characteristic defines what is "in" or "out" in a given situation, the theory rests on the assumption that people generally prefer their own. However, Simmel argues that meaningful social relationships can happen between people from different groups if the people are similar in many other ways (i.e., if their other social circles substantially intersect). These shared commonalities become the grounds on which social relationships can be formed despite belonging to different groups.

Blau adds to Simmel's concept by arguing that various structural factors influence opportunities to satisfy in-group preferences, making intergroup relations more likely under certain conditions and less likely under others. The probability of intergroup relations depends on a few key factors. First and most importantly, the number of characteristics in common between members of two different groups affects and is affected by meaningful exposure to each other. Furthermore, the more characteristics in common, the less the one unshared characteristic matters. Second, equality affects the numerical availability of in-group options that share other characteristics. When there are less in-group individuals of similar status on other characteristics, there are proportionately more out-group individuals of otherwise similar status.

A third element, group size, plays a role within each of these other key factors. As preliminarily validated in the Jackson, Mississippi example, a smaller percentage of Blacks seem to identify as also White when the Black group size is large. But why? Numerically large minority groups tend to be geographically and socially segregated (Blalock 1967; Massey and Denton 1993; Waters 1999; Wilson 1980). These groups become homogenous and delineated, limiting contact and the extent any characteristics are shared with members of the out-group (Blau 1980; Castles and Miller 2003; Qian, Glick and Batson 2012; Sassen 2001, 2006; Waters 1999). Even when a large minority group is not as homogenous and delineated, such as in cities where there is greater equality between racial groups, the group is composed of amply sized stratification tiers to adequately offer plenty of same-race, same-status options. That is, equality creates conditions that provide adequately sized in-group relationship opportunities with members of similar status, assuming the group size is large. In both cases, the theory maintains that intergroup relations are less likely among members of large groups. And in this chapter, I test whether the same line of reasoning extends beyond inter-racial marriage to interracial identification.

Meanwhile, a larger proportion of Blacks identify as also White when the Black group size is small. We saw this preliminarily validated in the Coeur d'Alene, Idaho, example. Whether a small racial group is homogeneous or heterogenous, there are numerically more relationship options outside the group. In the pages that follow, I test whether the same reasoning extends beyond marriages between Blacks and Whites, to racial identification with both Blacks and Whites.

Blau's macrostructural theory of intergroup relations can utilize most any demographic variable to distinguish groups (e.g., religion, class, age). In the twenty-first-century United States, the theory clearly lends itself to race as a dominating demographic characteristic still defining what is in-group and what is out-group. The theory has been used to explain the probability of several different types of interracial relations including interracial contact, conflict, and marriage. The postulates tested include those centered on demo-graphic consolidation (i.e., the extent race is correlated with several other characteristics at once, which would limit one's exposure to members of other races), inequality, and group size.

Demographic Consolidation among Blacks

The theory contends that relations can happen between members of different races if most of their other social circles intersect. Race, however, often has strong correlations with many other characteristics, thereby inhibiting the chances that members of two racial groups significantly share other types of social circles. Heightened racial salience, intolerance of dissimilar others, and antagonistic allegiance in opposition to institutional and interpersonal racism have a way of consolidating sociodemographic characteristics and homog-enizing the minority group (Blau 1980; Castles and Miller 2003; Qian et al. 2012; Sassen 2001, 2006; Waters 1999). Under these conditions, interracial relations are less likely to build because social circles for members of differ-ent racial groups don't intersect.

Residential segregation best operationalizes this concept (Anderson and Saenz 1994; Kalmijn 1998; Kalmijn and Van Tubergen 2010). Segregation limits the number of similarities between racial groups because geographical confinement creates cultural and social barriers by consolidating character-istics that would otherwise vary (e.g., employment opportunities, healthcare system access, and religious denomination attendance). That is, residential segregation has a way of completely segregating racial groups in a multitude of ways beyond simply separating domiciles (Massey and Denton 1993; Qian et al. 2012). The effect is especially compounded in cities where the racial minority group is numerically large, as larger racial minority groups are more likely to be perceived as a threat to the majority group (Blalock 1967; Massey and Denton 1993; Waters 1999; Wilson 1980).

When segregation limits social operations to immediate neighborhoods, quality contact with the majority group is rare (Fitzpatrick and Hwang 1992). Without regular opportunities for contact, commonalities, or interpersonal respect, interracial relations are arguably less likely (Blau 1994). But when race is less correlated with the distribution of other sociodemographic characteristics, the racial minority group is more exposed to the majority group on common ground and interracial relations is consistently found to be more likely (Anderson and Saenz 1994; Blau 1994; Blau, Beeker and Fitzpatrick 1984; Blau and Schwartz 1984; Blum 1984, 1985; Fitzpatrick and Hwang 1992; Heaton and Jacobson 2000; Lichter 2013; Qian 1999; Qian et al. 2012; Skvoretz 1990). I expect the same principles to hold true for interracial identification, especially among Blacks identifying as also White, as Blacks are the racial minority group most persistently segregated from Whites for the longest period of time in the United States.

Inequality between Blacks and Whites

The theory assumes people prefer to interact with members of their own racial group, so long as they are similar in most other ways as well (Blau 1977; see also Kalmijn and Van Tubergen 2010; Simmel 1908). However, there are certain conditions limiting the numerical availability of same-race associates who also share other characteristics. The likelihood of interracial relations is increased when the proportion of same-status, different-race options is considerably larger than the proportion of same-status, same-race options.

The effect of one's status in intergroup relations studies is often operationalized through (in)equality measurements because relationships depend on commonalities forged on the basis of equality (Blau 1977; Lichter 2013). Blau (1977) defines *inequality* as the relative difference between two groups on an interval-measured variable. The theory implies preference for education (over income or socioeconomic status indicators) for this role. Rytina et al. (1988) statistically confirm that education is the most suitable inequality measure for use in testing this theory, arguing the volatility of income can't compete with the stable status associated with education.

The relative difference between racial groups on educational attainment affects interracial relations in different ways. On the one hand, when more racial minorities have access to higher education, the salience of race is reduced (Blau 1977, 1994; Broman, Neighbors and Jackson 1998; Croll 2007; Kalmijn 1993; Qian et al. 2012). Shared non-race characteristics and interests become more interpersonally relevant, making interracial relationships more likely (Blum 1984; Gans 2007; Harris 2002; Heaton and Jacobson 2000; Lichter 2013; McPherson, Smith-Lovin and Cook 2001; Qian 1997, 1999). On the other hand, increased upward mobility puts greater proportions of racial minorities in higher rung positions and, assuming the minority group size is adequate, increases the available pool of same-status, same-race suitors (Blau 1977, 1994). As such, decreasing racial inequality at the macro-level actually decreases interracial relation likelihood despite decreased social distance at the interpersonal level (Blau 1994; Blau et al. 1984; Blau et al. 1982; Rytina et al. 1988).

In the pages that follow, I test whether these concepts also hold true for individuals identifying with two races over identifying with one. I expect they will, and that the magnitude of the relationship will be greatest for biracial Blacks identifying as also White, as Blacks are the racial minority group most persistently oppressed from equality with Whites in the United States.

Group Size of Blacks, Relative to Whites

The theory concludes that interracial relations are more likely among members of groups that are numerically small relative to the majority group size because numerically limited in-group options make out-group options statistically more probable. The effect is particularly apparent in race applications because smaller racial groups tend to be more heterogeneous and therefore more distributed across various social dimensions than larger racial groups. That is, smaller racial groups are more likely to be characterized by more variation in economic standing, educational attainment, career fields and industries, and so forth. Such stratification would mean that there would be fewer same-race marriage partner options that also share similar economic standing, educational attainment, and so on, and therefore greater different-race marriage partner options that do share these other things in common.

Because smaller racial groups are more likely to share multiple non-race characteristics, interests, and activities in common venues with members of other racial groups, interracial relations are more likely (Blau 1977, 1994; Blau and Schwartz 1984; Frey and Farley 1996; Heaton and Jacobson 2000; Qian 1999). Furthermore, upwardly mobile minorities from smaller racial groups are more likely to intermarry despite greater educational equality because the selection pool of same-status, same-race suitors is still numerically limited (Blau 1994; Heaton and Jacobson 2000; Kalmijn 1998; Qian et al. 2012; St. John and Clymer 2000). That is, small groups are an exception to the uniquely macro-level phenomenon where increasing equality decreases interracial relations. Again, at micro- and meso-levels of analysis, greater educational equality tends to facilitate interracial marriage, but at the macro-level, group size interferes and paradoxically turns the relationship negative.

Structural factors such as demographic consolidation, inequality, and group size have repeatedly been shown to affect the likelihood of relations with different-race others. Most tests have focused on interracial marriage, in part because of the availability of large-scale, quantitative data of sufficient sample size (Blau 1994). Indeed, over 13 percent of today's legal marriages are interracial (Lee and Bean 2007b). In addition, "marriage is undoubtedly the most profound and lasting human relation of all those voluntarily established" (Blau et al. 1984:591). Friendships on the other hand tend to fleeting and situational; they change much more frequently over the life course and across different situations within life course segments. And the number of friends one can have at once is really only limited by practicality. Interracial crime is another form of intergroup relations, but is even more fleeting and volatile than friendships. As such, interracial marriage has continued to be the most suitable type of intergroup relation for evaluating the effect of structural influences on racial integration because of its durability and longevity, coupled with the availability of large-scale, quantitative data.

Contemporary American society, however, is characterized by widespread cohabitation, partnerships not legally recognized as marriage, divorce, and non-marital childbearing. Black-White biracial couples are 1.7 times more likely to cohabitate than marry (Kalmijn 1993; Lichter and Qian 2005; Qian et al. 2012), more likely to divorce (Zhang and Van Hook 2009), and more likely to produce children out of wedlock (Kalmijn 1993) than same-race couples. Although biracial Blacks are more likely to share heritage with Whites than any other race, Blacks and Whites are the least likely groups to marry each other (Edmonston, Lee and Passel 2002; Heaton and Jacobson 2000; Qian 1997) and experience more social distance than any other racial pairing (Qian 1999). Interracial marriage incidence has commonly been used to indicate racial distance (Fu and Heaton 2000; Kalmijn 1998; Kalmijn and Van Tubergen 2010; Lee and Bean 2004; Lichter and Qian 2005; Qian et al. 2012; Suro 1999; Zhang and Vanhook 2009), however its footing as a preferred racial integration indicator is becoming less steady (Brunsma 2005).

The flexibility of the new census race question more accurately tallies variations in racial groups than ever before. This gives demographers the opportunity to utilize data on biracial *people*, rather than biracial *marriage*, as an emerging social distance indicator (Bean and Stevens 2003; Bratter 2007; Lee and Bean 2004). In the same way interracial marriage has reflected racial integration in the past, biracial identification may represent a more salient indicator of integration in today's society (Kalmijn 1993).

FACTORS AFFECTING BLACK-WHITE
INTERRACIAL IDENTIFICATION

Considerable quantitative advancements have been made identifying various determinants of multiracial identification. These studies examine the influence of sociodemographic and social psychological factors at micro- and meso-levels. Educational attainment generally encourages multiracial identification (Brunsma 2005; Croll 2007; Masuoka 2011; Roth 2005; Tafoya, Johnson and Hill 2005) with some exception (Bratter 2007; Hochschild and Weaver 2007). Immigrant status tends to discourage multiracial identification (Bean and Stevens 2003; Masuoka 2011; Roth 2005; Tafoya et al. 2005). Contextual factors such as discrimination discourage multiracial identification (Brunsma 2005; Harris 2002; Hochschild and Weaver 2007; Masuoka 2011; Tafoya 2002; Tafoya et al. 2005), while neighborhood diversity encourages multiracial identification (Bratter 2007; Croll 2007; Harris 2002; Masuoka 2011; Tafoya et al. 2005). Trends vary by region (Bean and Stevens 2003; Croll 2007; Harris and Sim 2002; Masuoka 2011; Rockquemore and Brunsma 2008; Roth 2005) and racial group (Bratter 2007; Campbell 2007; Masuoka 2011; Roth 2005).

These types of sociodemographic and social psychological factors generally affect Black racial identification more than they affect racial identification among other racial minority groups in at least three ways. For one, Blacks experience greater degrees of sociodemographic inequality from Whites. Therefore, if the magnitude of the input variables (e.g., educational attainment) is stronger for Blacks than, say, Asians, the effect on the output variable (lower likelihood of racially identifying with Whites) is going to be stronger. Indeed, Blacks experience more discrimination (especially in the educational system) than Asians and are therefore less likely than Asians to identify as also White.

Secondly, social psychological factors affect Black racial identification more than Asian racial identification because there have been longer, more established norms around racially classifying Blacks in America. Hypodescents commands that biracial individuals default to the identity of their minority half (Davis 1991) and this phenomenon presumably extends to racial identification. But Blacks are held to this norm considerably more than other racial groups. For example, Asian-Whites are equally as likely to be identified as monoracial White as they are to be identified as monoracial Asian or biracial Asian-White (Roth 2005; Xie and Goyette 1997). When forced to choose one race, biracial Black-Whites usually default to Black while biracial Asian-Whites usually default to White (Tafoya et al. 2005).

Finally, sociodemographic and social psychological factors also influence how the parents of biracial children choose to identify their children. Once again, trends differ by race. Asians married in America are roughly five times more likely to marry someone from another racial group than Black Americans. This sociodemographic insight suggests that the likelihood of children identifying as biracial is less likely for Blacks than Asians (as shown in table 2.1). The parent's educational attainment also affects the likelihood of identifying biracial children as such, again affecting different racial groups differently. Whereas more educated Black-White couples are more likely to assign their children as biracial, more educated Asian-White couples are more likely to assign their children as monoracial Asian (Roth 2005). Furthermore, among parents that are themselves multiracial, a child with a Black multiracial parent is less likely to be classified as multiracial than a child with a non-Black multiracial parent (Bratter 2007). Adding further to the complexity, a multiracial Black child's likelihood of being identified as multiracial changes dramatically with age (Roth 2005). As biracial Black-White children age, their likelihood of being classified as biracial decreases significantly. The same is not necessarily true for Asians (Xie and Goyette 1997).

These quantitative studies examining the influence of sociodemographic and social psychological factors on individual-level (and sometimes house-hold-level or even group-level) units of analysis confirm what qualitative work has been yielding for many years—racial identity is extraordinarily complex (and racial identification is no exception). On the one hand, weighty hypodescent norms command cut and dry racial identification for Blacks. But on the other hand, these studies find that racial identification is more conditional on certain sociodemographic and social psychological factors for Blacks than it is for other racial groups, especially among Blacks who are half White.

Much like empiricism on biracial marriage and other forms of interracial relations, biracial identification empiricism gravitates toward the Black-White divide. Methodological convenience from large sample sizes aside, Blacks and Whites are important groups to study together for many reasons. These two groups experience more social, cultural, and spatial distance than any other racial pairing (Bean and Stevens 2003; Bratter 2007; Gans 2007; Lee and Bean 2004, 2007a, 2007b; Lichter and Qian 2005; Massey and Denton 1993; Qian 1997, 1999). As such, Blacks and Whites are the least likely groups to marry each other (Edmonston et al. 2002; Heaton and Jacobson 2000; Lichter and Qian 2005; Masuoka 2011; Qian 1997).

While biracial Blacks are more likely to share heritage with Whites than any other racial group, Blacks with recent multiracial heritage are the least likely multiracial group to claim multiracial identification in the first place (Bratter 2007; Lee and Bean 2007b; Loveman and Muniz 2007; Parker et al. 2004; Roth 2005). Despite ancestral awareness (Davis 1991; Spencer 1997),

Blacks are more likely to rely on social construction (e.g., the legacy of slavery in the United States, the one-drop rule, systemic and persistent discrimination) than genealogy in the self-identification process (Lee and Bean 2007a, 2007b). Blacks have at times wielded Black monoracial identification to show solidarity in the face of racism (Hochschild and Weaver 2007). As a result, Blacks are more likely to identify monoracially than any other racial minority.

The iconoclasts claiming Black-White biracial identification are therefore of considerable substantive interest, hence the preponderance of quality empiricism analyzing these individuals. There is uncharted opportunity, however, for analyzing how differences between macrostructural contexts influence how these individuals racially identify. Knowing that structural constraints affect intimate social relationship choices, and trends in biracial identification mirror biracial marriage patterns, this chapter applies concepts drawn from Blau's macrostructural theory on interracial marriage to Black biracial identification with Whites.

Marrying-in (in the theory and accompanying interracial marriage studies) refers to Blacks marrying Blacks, and marrying-out refers to Blacks choosing a partner from another racial group. I define the equivalent construct in the biracial identification analysis that follows similarly, where in-group identification is sticking with the status quo—identifying as monoracially Black, and out-group identification is choosing to identify as also White.

HYPOTHESIZING THE INFLUENCE OF STRUCTURE ON BLACK BIRACIAL IDENTIFICATION WITH WHITES

The theory assumes that smaller groups experience less discrimination and inequality, and proposes two key postulates. First, cities with less discrimination facilitate opportunities for healthy interracial exposure. Second, cities with less inequality increase social mobility for racial minorities. This helps break down racial stereotypes and helps to close the social distance gap between racial groups. However, increased upward mobility puts greater proportions of racial minorities in higher rung positions and, assuming adequate group size, actually increases the pool of same-status, same-race marriage partner options, facilitating healthy interracial exposure but increasing the likelihood of same-race intimate relations.

Factors facilitating interracial marriage may also encourage interracial identification. It is hypothesized that the same parameters influencing interracial marriage also influence interracial identification. Hence,

H_1. The more social circles between Blacks and Whites intersect, the greater the likelihood Blacks will report biracial identification with Whites.

H_2. The greater the educational equality between Blacks and Whites, the greater the likelihood Blacks will report monoracial Black identification.

H_3. The smaller the Black group size relative to Whites, the greater the likelihood Blacks will report biracial identification with Whites.

DATA AND METHODS

Social structure is embodied by multidimensional social arrangements between proximal groups (Blau 1994). In the United States, diverse populations living in close proximity characterize urban centers (McPherson et al. 2001). Metropolitan areas have been the primary pallet for interracial contact since the antebellum period (Wilson 1980). Therefore, MSAs and New England city and town areas (NECTAs) are natural units of analysis for measuring interracial contact and, conceivably, interracial identification. There are 363 metropolitan areas in the continental United States. All are used in the analysis that follows.

Dependent Variable: Black-White
Biracial Identification Incidence

The theory asks, "Why do some groups have more extensive intergroup relations than others?" (Blau 1977:20). Blau asserts that macrostructural forces such as demographic consolidation, inequality, and relative group size work together to facilitate or constrain opportunities for relationship development between members of two different groups. "The criterion of intergroup relations is the rate of dyadic relations of persons in one social position with those in other social positions, for example, the proportion of Catholics whose best friend is a Protestant" (Blau 1994:22). Blau operationalizes the dependent variable with *intermarriage incidence* defined as the proportion of members in one group whose spouse is not a member of the same group (Blau and Schwartz 1984). Subsequent empiricism follows suit (e.g., Anderson and Saenz 1994; Blau 1994; Blau, Beeker and Fitzpatrick 1984; Rytina et al. 1988).

The analysis in this book examines whether similar principles can help explain why some groups have more extensive intergroup identification than others. And for the first time in U.S. history, the 2000 Census allowed residents to mark more than one racial choice. This policy was continued in 2010. The 2010 U.S. Census race question offered several options for self-identification: White; Black, African American, or Negro; American Indian or Alaska Native; multiple Asian ethnicities; multiple Pacific Islander ethnicities; and Some Other Race. Respondents checked as many categories as they wished. The Bureau then collapsed counts from the many Asian ethnicities into one category called "Asian," and combined "Native Hawaiian" with "Other Pacific Islander." The Bureau then tabulated and reported on these six racial categories: White; Black, African American, or Negro; American Indian or Alaska Native; Asian; Native Hawaiian and Other Pacific Islander; and Some Other Race. Respondents are considered monoracial if they identified with only one of these six categories, and biracial if they identified with two of these six categories. (Respondents indicating three or more of these six categories are also tabulated by the Bureau, but are outside the scope of this analysis.)

In addition to the six major racial groups, the census also acknowledges two ethnicities: Hispanic, and non-Hispanic. This analysis focuses on biracial individuals without consideration of Hispanicity for two reasons. First, this study combines Hispanic and non-Hispanic for the sake of analytical consistency because data for all independent variables are not available by both race and Hispanicity. Second, separating Hispanic from Non-Hispanic biracial groups would compromise sample size among smaller biracial groups in certain metropolitan areas.

Note that this approach implies self-identification despite the sample including underage Americans whose parent or guardian fills out the census form on their behalf. Rather than decreasing the sample size by limiting the analysis to adults, this study assumes that the self-identification process and the structural dynamics influencing that decision extends to the process of adults identifying the race of minors in their household. I also make the assumption that the way minors are identified by guardians is closely related to the way those minors identify themselves at the time of enumeration and how they will identify themselves as adults—an assumption supported by other scholars working in this field (Rockquemore and Brunsma 2002; Roth 2005; Xie and Goyette 1997).

Using data from Census Summary File 1, the dependent variable is calculated as a count of individuals identifying with two particular racial groups, Black and White, divided by a count of all the individuals identifying with the racial minority of those two groups. In this case, that's a count of biracial individuals who indicate both Black and White, divided by the count of the entire Black population. This is interpreted as the percentage of Blacks who are half White. For each city, the number of Blacks reporting monoracial and biracial identification with Whites is calculated. Although the ratio of Blacks to Whites is 0.18, only 4.4 percent of Blacks claim biracial identification with Whites. Metropolitan areas range from 0.6 percent claiming Black-White identification in Jackson, Mississippi, (where Blacks represent 48.2 percent of the population) to 42.2 percent in Coeur d'Alene, Idaho (where Blacks represent but 0.7 percent of the population).

Independent Variables: Structural Factors
Affecting Blacks and Whites

Blau (1977) theorizes that key macrostructural variables explain why some racial groups have higher incidence of interracial relations than others. These include interracial exposure (as the opposite of demographic consolidation that is so characteristic of racial segregation), racial equality (as the opposite of inequality), and Black group size relative to Whites. Here I test whether those same variables can also explain why some cities witness higher incidence of Black biracial identification with Whites than others.

Black Exposure to Whites

Blau (1977) assumes that the probability of intergroup relations depends on the spatial and social distance between two groups and their opportunities for contact with one another. Simply put, the number of characteristics in common between members of two different groups affects the likelihood of relationship development. This is because the more characteristics in common, which Blau calls *intersection*, the less the one unshared characteristic (i.e., race) matters. *Consolidation*, which is the inverse of intersection, is the degree to which race is correlated with several other demographic characteristics at once. Blau and Schwartz (1984) operationalize this concept by calculating demographic consolidation as the average of correlations between race and other demographic characteristics such as occupation, industry, birth region, and mother tongue. Small average correlations mean that racial groups intersect; they have multiple characteristics in common. Large average correlations mean that racial groups are consolidated; they have little in common with other racial groups. Blau et al. (1984), Blau and Schwartz (1984), and Blau (1994) find that interracial relations decrease with consolidation and increase with intersection. In this study, it is similarly expected that characteristics in common with multiple races affect identification with multiple races.

Based on Blau's (1977) theoretical assumption that the probability of intergroup relations depends on the spatial and social distance between two groups and their opportunities for contact with one another, many empiricists have recommended replacing the multiple correlation measure employed by Blau, with a single measure of segregation (Anderson and Saenz 1994; Blum 1984; Fitzpatrick and Hwang 1992; Heaton and Jacobson 2000; Kalmijn 1998; Kalmijn and Van Tubergen 2010; Lieberson and Waters 1988; Peach 1980; South and Messner 1986; Stevens and Swicegood 1987). Racial segregation stifles the extent to which demographic and lifestyle characteristics are free to vary. This homogenization of characteristics, coupled with geographic, cultural, and social delineation from the rest of society, severely limits Black exposure to Whites. If racial segregation hinders interracial relationships, it may also hinder interracial identification. Neighborhood exposure, on the other hand, influences opportunities for interracial interaction (Marsden 1990; Peach 1996; St. John and Clymer 2000), interracial marriage (Anderson and Saenz 1994; Blau et al. 1984; Blau and Schwartz 1984; Blum 1984, 1985; Fitzpatrick and Hwang 1992; Heaton and Jacobson 2000; Lichter 2013; Qian 1999; Qian et al. 2012), and biracial identification (Xie and Goyette 1997).

Racial segregation can be measured in different ways, such as by examining the evenness of racial group distribution across a residential area, or through the degree of exposure one racial group has to another (Massey and Denton 1988, 1989). Fitzpatrick and Hwang (1992) argue that the exposure dimension of segregation follows the spirit of Blau's theory much more closely than the evenness dimension, and Anderson and Saenz (1994) subsequently concur. Indeed, Hwang, Saenz, and Aguirre (1994), as well as South and Messner (1986), use the dissimilarity index to measure the evenness dimension of segregation. But they end up with non-statistically significant results.

In this chapter, the exposure index of segregation is used to measure the probability of interaction between Blacks and Whites (Population Studies Center 2013). This index measures the probability of interaction between one group and another by taking the average percentage of an area that is group-a, within the neighborhood (i.e., census tract) of a group-b person. Neighborhood compositions are listed for average White persons, Black persons, Asian persons, and Hispanic persons in the United States by the average percentage of each area that is White, Black, American Indian/Alaskan Native, Hawaiian/Pacific Islander, other race, two or more races, or Hispanic. The theoretical framework leveraged in this paper is concerned with the relationship between a majority group and a minority group. In this case, I'm concerned with the exposure Blacks have to Whites in order to see how this influences the percentage of Blacks that biracially identify as also White. As such I do not take the inverse (i.e., the average percentage of an area that is Black, within the neighborhood of a White person). Rather, I take the index that measures the probability of interaction between Blacks and Whites by taking the average percentage of an area that is White, within the neighborhood (i.e., census tract) of a Black American person. The exposure index for each metropolitan area can theoretically range from 0 (indicating no exposure between Blacks and Whites) to a number equal to the proportion of the population that is White in a city with only one Black person. An exposure score calculated from 2010 Census data for each metropolitan area is available from the University of Michigan Population Studies Center. Scores for Black exposure to Whites range from 4.8 in Laredo, Texas, to 94.2 in Parkersburg-Marietta-Vienna, West Virginia-Ohio.

Racial Equality between Blacks and Whites

Blau (1977) assumes that the probability of intergroup relations depends on the social distance between two groups and their opportunities for contact with one another. The inverse of this would assume that the probability of intergroup relations also depends on social stratification within the group. That is, the availability of within-group associates that share other characteristics (i.e., social status) decreases the likelihood of interracial relations. In contrast, when there are less same-race individuals of similar status, there are proportionately more different-race individuals of similar status.

Equality in college education has consistently been shown to influence interracial marriage (Lichter 2013; Qian et al. 2012). Similarly, it is expected in this study that the same phenomenon affects an individual's likelihood to identify with multiple races and will therefore affect the proportion of racial minorities identifying biracially in each city. When there are fewer racial minorities of otherwise similar status, there are proportionately more majority race individuals of similar status; this preponderance of different-race but same-status individuals arguably affects the likelihood a racial minority will identify with that second race.

This difference in distribution between two groups across social positions is measured on a status-predicting demographic dimension such as income or education (Blau 1977). Blau and Schwartz (1984) operationalize inequality using education, family income, personal income, earnings, and occupational status or socioeconomic status (SEI). However, Rytina et al. (1988) argue that education is the best measure for quantifying structural inequality because income is volatile; once educational credentials are acquired, they cannot be lost. Blau stands by this position in the final revision of the theory (1994). This empiricism finds that as educational inequality between races increases, so too do interracial relations (Blau 1994; Blau and Schwartz 1984; Rytina et al. 1988).

Blau and Schwartz (1984) recommend relative measures of inequality rather than absolute measures of inequality because proportionate differences are independent of the mean, which assuredly differs between racial groups. Empiricists generally follow this advice, but the specific calculation tends to depend on the data set used. For example, Blau and Schwartz (1984), Rytina et al. (1988), and Blau (1994) use the Gini coefficient because their data count years of education on a ratio scale.

In this study, educational attainment is available from the 2007–2011 ACS Table C15002. The respondent was asked, "What is the highest degree or level of school this person has completed?" Response categories included the following: no schooling completed, nursery school, kindergarten, grade one to eleven, twelfth grade no diploma, regular high school diploma, GED or alternative credential, some college credit but less than one year of college credit, one or more years of college credit no degree, associate's degree, bachelor's degree, master's degree, professional degree, and doctorate degree. Population counts by race are provided in the following categories for adults 25 years of age and older in each metropolitan area: less than high school diploma, high school graduate/GED, some college or associate's degree, and bachelor's degree or higher. Allocation rates (i.e., percent of educational attainment questions with missing data or bearing invalid answers for which statistical imputation procedures were performed) are within acceptable ranges. Between 2007 and 2011, 5.6 percent or fewer education attainment responses had to be statistically imputed. This figure is considered reasonable; reliability is not generally called into question until missing data exceeds 10 percent (Dong and Peng 2013).

Because race and education are both categorical variables, chi-square is used to test the independence between the two. For each metropolitan area in the 2007–2011 ACS, chi-square is calculated for the relationship between race and education by dividing the raw chi-square term by the maximum chi-square value (and then multiplying by 100). Because chi-square indicates the extent census frequencies deviate from what would be expected if race and education were independent, higher scores indicate greater deviation from independence between race and education, implying educational attainment is more dependent upon race. Therefore, the calculated expression is subtracted from 100 to reverse the scale such that higher scores indicate greater educational parity (i.e., education is less dependent on race) between two racial groups. Scores range from 0.00 in Coeur d'Alene, Idaho, where race and education are highly dependent on one another, to 8.65 in Greenville, North Carolina, where race and education are more independent among Blacks and Whites.

Black Group Size Relative to Whites

Blau's theory assumes relative group size affects both exposure and equality (Blau 1977, 1994; Blau and Schwartz 1984). In regard to interracial exposure, numerically large minority groups tend to be geographically and socially segregated (Blalock 1967; Massey and Denton 1993; Waters 1999; Wilson 1980). These groups become homogenous and delineated, limiting contact and the extent any characteristics are shared with another racial group (Blau 1980; Castles and Miller 2003; Qian, Glick and Batson 2012; Sassen 2001, 2006; Waters 1999). In contrast, equality creates conditions that provide adequately sized same-race relationship opportunities with members of similar status unless the minority group is small (Blau 1977, 1994). In both cases, interracial relations are more likely among members of small groups.

Because it is assumed, Blau doesn't explicitly test group size alongside the two key theorems (i.e., consolidation/exposure and inequality/equality) in his final model (1994). However, most empirical tests of Blau's theory not only control group size but consider it a key theorem (Anderson and Saenz 1994; Butts 2008; Fitzpatrick and Hwang 1992; Heaton and Jacobson 2000; Qian 1999). In fact, group size is the single most tested component of Blau's theory. Empiricism almost unanimously finds relative group size statistically significant and negatively related to interracial marriage as theorized (Fitzpatrick and Hwang 1992; Heaton and Jacobson 2000; Hwang et al. 1994, 1997; Qian 1999; Qian et al. 2012). Clearly, interracial relations are more likely among members of small groups.

Similarly, I expect interracial identification to also be more likely among members of small groups. Because this research analyzes percentages of biracial persons rather than monoracial persons in biracial relationships, I measure relative group size by calculating the proportion of monoracial and multiracial minorities associated with one racial group to 1,000 monoracial majority group members. Group size is measured as the number of Blacks per 1,000 single-race Whites. Data for this calculation is available for each MSA in Census Summary File 1. The ratio of Blacks to 1,000 Whites ranges from 5.8 in Laredo, Texas, to 535.1 in Albany, Georgia.

Control Variables

Other variables isolate structural features examined in Blau's theory and subsequent empirical tests. These include the percentage of the Black population that is foreign-born and the geographic region.

The percentage of the Black population foreign-born is controlled because areas with larger foreign-born populations tend to have more interracial marriage (Blau 1994) and larger biracial populations (Wright et al. 2003). Immigrants can be more likely to intermarry than their ancestral counterparts in the origin (Qian 1999). Note that this may not be the case among those who immigrate in pursuit of higher education, as they often arrive with focal families (Castles and Miller 2003). Furthermore, immigrant presence can enhance diversity tolerance and further immigrant influx (Lee and Bean 2004). Additionally, differing race classification constructions (Masuoka

2011; Tafoya, Johnson and Hill 2005) and racial identities among foreign-born populations in reaction to American-born people of color (Waters 1999) must be isolated.

Additionally, foreign-born racial minorities immigrate to the United States with different understandings of what it even means to be a racial minority than American-born minorities and second-generation immigrants of color (Waters 1999). Indeed, immigrant status tends to discourage multiracial identification (Bean and Stevens 2003; Masuoka 2011; Roth 2005; Tafoya et al. 2005). Higher employment (Wilson 1980) and the effect of immigration on inequality (Blau 1977, 1994) can set foreign-born Blacks particularly apart from their native-born racial counterparts. Controlling for nativity helps avoid confounding effects from differing exposure opportunities (Peach 1996), as well as contrasting historical contexts between Blacks and Whites.

Five-year estimates of the number of foreign-born Blacks are available from the 2007–2011 ACS Table B16005. Question 7 asked, "Where was this person born?" with two response options: "In the United States" with a space to indicate the state, or "Outside the United States" with a space to indicate the country. Allocation rates (i.e., percentage of place of birth questions with missing data or bearing invalid answers for which statistical imputation procedures were performed) are within acceptable ranges. Between 2007 and 2011, 7.0 percent or fewer responses were statistically imputed. This figure is considered reasonable; reliability is not generally called into question until missing data exceeds 10 percent (Dong and Peng 2013).

For each city, the percentage of the racial minority group that is foreign-born is calculated by taking a count of foreign-born minorities in a given racial group, in this case Black, and dividing by a count of the total population in that minority group. Percentages can range from 0 to 100. The percentage of Blacks that are foreign-born ranges from 0.0 percent where are there no reported foreign-born Blacks in Sandusky, Ohio, Kokomo, Indiana, and Coeur d'Alene, Idaho, to 60.4 percent in Fargo, North Dakota-Minnesota.

Note that an MSA is a geographic delineation defined by the Census Bureau. At its core is an urban center with a population of at least 50,000. Surrounding areas outside the city limits are included as part of the metro if there is a large enough proportion of people and commerce interacting with that urban center. Simply put, an MSA is a market, and it includes people who also live outside the city if there are significant commuting patterns from those surrounding areas into the urban center. Outer boundaries of an MSA follow county lines. So although there may be heavy commuting patterns into the urban center from only part of a county, the full county is included in the MSA. And although counties do not cross state lines, some border-cities, like Fargo, include counties from the adjacent state in the broader MSA.

Blau (1977) acknowledges that regional variations shape interracial relations and therefore must be controlled. The effects of regional variation on interracial relations persist beyond the effects of exposure, equality, and group size due to racial identification strength, group allegiance, and solidarity (Blum 1984; Brunsma 2005; Croll 2007; Fitzpatrick and Hwang 1992; Heaton and Jacobson 2000; Hochschild and Weaver 2007; Qian 1999; Tucker and Mitchell-Kernan 1990). Racial salience can be more influential than other variables, especially when it comes to the tolerance of intimate interracial relationships (Blum 1984; Heaton and Jacobson 2000; McPherson et al. 2001; Schwartz 1990). This study assumes the same may be true of interracial identification, therefore region must be controlled.

I designated the South as the comparison group for Blacks for several reasons. First, the literature supports the South as "different" for Blacks. For example, the South is particularly distinguished from non-South regions by its means of production, politico-cultural institutions, and other contemporary ramifications of historical impact on Blacks (Wilson 1980). Second, the Exposure Index of segregation finds Blacks most separated from both Whites and Asians in the South. Third, the majority of Blacks live in the South (50.9 percent). Additionally, the average size of the Black population relative to Whites across metropolitan areas in each region is greatest in the South. Furthermore, the percentage of Blacks claiming biracial White is lowest in the South. And finally, fifteen of the sixteen states still observing anti-miscegenation laws as late as 1967 were in the South.

The regional classification of each metropolitan area is available from Census Summary File 1. There are four regions defined by the Census Bureau: West, Midwest, South, and Northeast. The continental West includes California, Oregon, Washington, Idaho, Montana, Wyoming, Nevada, Utah, Colorado, Arizona, and New Mexico. The Midwest includes North Dakota, South Dakota, Nebraska, Kansas, Minnesota, Iowa, Missouri, Wisconsin, Illinois, Indiana, Ohio, and Michigan. The South includes Texas, Oklahoma, Arkansas, Louisiana, Mississippi, Alabama, Florida, Georgia, South Carolina, North Carolina, Virginia, West Virginia, Tennessee, Kentucky, Maryland, and Delaware. The Northeast includes Pennsylvania, New Jersey, New York, Rhode Island, Connecticut, Massachusetts, Vermont, New Hampshire, and Maine. Regions are coded into a dummy variable where the West, Midwest, and Northeast are coded as 1, and the South is coded as 0 to indicate the reference group.

Analytic Design

OLS regression is used to analyze these data once natural log transformations are performed on all variables (except region[1]). Blau's final model (1994) logs all variables for four reasons. First, logging corrected non-linearity and skewness to the right. Second, logging helped standardize the effects of different sized metropolitan areas in the sample. Third, logging also standardized the different test variable scales in the model. Finally, logging circumvented the need for interaction terms. Once transformations were completed, these data meet regression assumptions. [Note that some multicollinearity is typical among structural parameters. Similar to prior studies, bivariate correlations between explanatory variables are high but do not violate multicollinearity tests.]

STRUCTURAL INFLUENCE ON BLACK-WHITE BIRACIAL IDENTIFICATION

The correlation matrix and descriptive statistics for 363 metropolitan areas in the continental United States are shown in table 2.2. The untransformed average percentage of Blacks reporting Black-White biracial identification across these cities is 11.5 percent with 8.7 standard deviations, up from 7.1 percent, with 6.9 standard deviations in 2000 (Butts 2008). Coeur d'Alene Idaho, and Bend Oregon, have percentages greater than 3 standard deviations (i.e., means greater than 37.6 percent). Both cities are in the West where 19.7 percent of Blacks claim Black-White biracial identification, up from 12.8 percent in 2000 (Butts 2008). Nationally, 5.6 percent of Blacks in the South (up from 2.3 percent), 12.6 percent in the Northeast (up from 8.1 percent), and 13.7 percent in the Midwest (up from 8.8 percent) report biracial identification with Whites.

As shown in table 2.2, all explanatory variables correlate fairly strongly with the percentage of Blacks reporting Black-White biracial identification. This preliminarily supports the central research question; similar macrostructural variables known to influence biracial marriage appear to, at least at the bivariate level, also vary with biracial identification.

Bivariate Regression Analysis

The bivariate relationship between biracial identification incidence and each explanatory variable is displayed in table 2.3. Black exposure to Whites explains 42.9 percent of the geographical variation in the percentage of Blacks claiming Black-White biracial identification, racial equality explains 48.9 percent, and Black group size relative to Whites explains 80.0 percent. Consistent with interracial relations theory and intermarriage empiricism, Black exposure to Whites is related to biracial identification in a positive direction; greater Black exposure to Whites increases the percentage

Table 2.2 Correlations and Descriptive Statistics by Model

Model Variables	(1)	(2)	(3)	(4)	(5)	(6)	Mean	Standard Deviation
Black-White Model								
(1) Black-White Identification	1.000	-	-	-	-	-	-2.503	0.911
(2) Black Exposure to Whites	0.655**	1.000	-	-	-	-	3.967	0.403
(3) Racial Equality	-0.699**	-0.365**	1.000	-	-	-	-0.456	1.345
(4) Black Group Size	-0.894**	-0.483**	0.777**	1.000	-	-	4.331	1.043
(5) Foreign-Born Blacks	0.525**	0.187**	-0.322**	-0.524**	1.000	-	-3.110	1.340
(6) Region (Reference=South)	0.639**	0.268**	-0.291**	-0.519**	0.403**	1.000	0.592	0.492
Asian-White Model								
(1) Asian-White Identification	1.000	-	-	-	-	-	-1.943	0.393
(2) Asian Exposure to Whites	0.385**	1.000	-	-	-	-	4.221	0.307
(3) Racial Equality	-0.550**	-0.190**	1.000	-	-	-	-0.448	0.916
(4) Asian Group Size	-0.545**	-0.457**	0.487**	1.000	-	-	3.420	0.802
(5) Foreign-Born Asians	-0.158**	0.102	0.119*	-0.151**	1.000	-	-0.332	0.108
(6) Region (Reference=West)	-0.291**	0.226**	0.101	-0.315**	0.495**	1.000	0.790	0.409
Asian-Black Model								
(1) Asian-Black Identification	1.000	-	-	-	-	-	-4.425	0.710
(2) Asian Exposure to Blacks	0.704**	1.000	-	-	-	-	1.776	1.089
(3) Racial Equality	-0.439**	-0.300**	1.000	-	-	-	2.084	0.899
(4) Asian Group Size	-0.730**	-0.816**	0.260**	1.000	-	-	5.961	1.371
(5) Foreign-Born Asians	0.248**	0.376**	0.090	-0.417**	1.000	-	-0.332	0.108
(6) Region (Reference=West)	0.284**	0.584**	0.080	-0.659**	0.495**	1.000	0.788	0.409
Black-Asian Model								
(1) Black-Asian Identification	1.000	-	-	-	-	-	-5.567	0.877
(2) Black Exposure to Asians	0.645**	1.000	-	-	-	-	0.603	0.847
(3) Racial Equality	0.019	0.071	1.000	-	-	-	2.084	0.899
(4) Black Group Size	-0.812**	-0.685**	-0.281**	1.000	-	-	8.311	1.246
(5) Foreign-Born Blacks	0.595**	0.440**	0.269**	-0.649**	1.000	-	-3.110	1.340
(6) Region (Reference=South)	0.412**	0.266**	0.324**	-0.556**	0.403**	1.000	0.592	0.492

Source: Computed by author using data from Census (2010) and ACS (2007–2011).
Note n=363 MSAs.
*Correlation is significant at the 0.05 level (2-tailed).
**Correlation is significant at the 0.01 level (2-tailed).

Table 2.3 Macrostructural Effects on Biracial Identification by Model

Model Variables	Unstandardized Bivariate Statistics			Unstandardized Multivariate Statistics		
	Coeff.	S.E.	R^2	Coeff.	S.E.	R^2
Black-White Model						0.911
Black Exposure to Whites	1.482**	0.090	0.429	0.663**	0.041	
Racial Equality	−0.474**	0.025	0.489	−0.068***	0.018	
Black Group Size	−0.781**	0.021	0.800	−0.449***	0.028	
Foreign-Born Blacks	0.357**	0.030	0.275	0.050***	0.013	
Region (Reference=South)	1.182**	0.075	0.408	0.434**	0.035	
(Constant)			−	−3.324**	0.234	
Asian-White Model						0.611
Asian Exposure to Whites	0.491**	0.062	0.148	0.293**	0.048	
Racial Equality	−0.236**	0.019	0.303	−0.097***	0.017	
Asian Group Size	−0.267**	0.022	0.298	−0.235***	0.022	
Foreign-Born Asians	−0.572**	0.189	0.025	0.031	0.139	
Region (Reference=West)	−0.279**	0.048	0.085	−0.456**	0.039	
(Constant)			−	−2.049**	0.249	
Asian-Black Model						0.668
Asian Exposure to Blacks	0.459**	0.024	0.495	0.210**	0.035	
Racial Equality	−0.347**	0.037	0.193	−0.126***	0.028	
Asian Group Size	−0.378**	0.019	0.532	−0.320***	0.030	
Foreign-Born Asians	1.627**	0.335	0.061	0.267	0.235	
Region (Reference=West)	0.493**	0.088	0.081	−0.553***	0.079	
(Constant)			−	−2.103**	0.263	
Black-Asian Model						0.727
Black Exposure to Asians	0.668**	0.042	0.416	0.121**	0.040	
Racial Equality	0.019	0.051	0.000	−0.222***	0.029	
Black Group Size	−0.571**	0.022	0.659	−0.487***	0.036	
Foreign-Born Blacks	0.390**	0.028	0.354	0.100***	0.024	
Region (Reference=South)	0.734**	0.086	0.169	0.014	0.062	
(Constant)			−	−0.828**	0.322	

Source: Computed by author using data from Census (2010) and ACS (2007–2011).
Note n = 363 MSAs.
**Correlation is significant at the 0.01 level (2-tailed).

of Black biracial identification with Whites. Greater educational equality between Blacks and Whites decreases Black biracial identification with Whites. Lastly, group size is negatively related to biracial identification, just as the theory suggests. When Black group size is small, biracial identification prevalence is greater than when Black group size is large relative to Whites.

Both control variables are also statistically significant. The percentage of Blacks foreign-born is related to Black biracial identification with Whites in a positive direction. Meaning, cities that have greater percentages of Blacks foreign-born also have greater percentages of Black biracially White. Similar to findings on biracial marriage, Blacks outside the South are more likely to claim Black-White biracial identification. These bivariate results generally demonstrate stronger R^2 statistics and more statistically significant results than interracial marriage studies.

Multiple Regression Analysis

The simultaneous regression of biracial identification on explanatory variables is shown in table 2.3. All variables significantly contribute to biracial identification incidence. The full model accounts for 91.1 percent of the geographical variation in Black biracial identification with Whites.

The first hypothesis predicts that greater Black exposure to Whites elicits greater Black-White identification. Blau considers the extent to which race is correlated with other demographic and lifestyle characteristics to be the most important variable in the theory, and this is confirmed by the model. Exposure strongly performs as expected, even with the effects of educational equality, group size, nativity, and geographic region parsed away. Institutional and interpersonal racism known to provoke defiance and rejection of a partially White heritage is minimized when Blacks have more exposure to Whites; greater exposure may inspire greater identification with both groups, signifying less social distance between races. Conversely, when Black exposure to Whites is limited, monoracial Black identification is more prevalent, conceivably due to intense geographic, social, and cultural boundaries characteristic of residentially segregated communities.

The second hypothesis predicts metro areas with greater educational equality between Blacks and Whites will have fewer Blacks reporting biracial identification with Whites. Equality is related to biracial identification. If Blacks are represented in each educational attainment tier to the same degree as Whites, same-race unions among Blacks would be more likely because Blacks would have greater access to other same-status Blacks. But since Blacks are underrepresented in higher socioeconomic tiers due to inequality, chances for interracial contact on common ground are limited for all but the upwardly mobile (and upward mobility does not come easily for Blacks). Along the same line of reasoning, it is not surprising that Black-White equality in education decreases Black-White biracial identification.

The third hypothesis predicts that members of smaller Black groups are more likely to identify as half White. Consistent with biracial marriage studies where members of small racial groups are more likely to marry majority group members because same-race options are limited, biracial identification with Whites is more prevalent when Blacks make up a small proportion of the population relative to Whites. Conclusively, the hypothesis that Black group size is negatively related to Black-White biracial identification is confirmed.

The percentage of Blacks who are foreign-born is related to Black biracial identification with Whites in a positive direction. That is, cities with a larger percentage of Blacks who are foreign-born also have a larger percentage of Blacks who are half White. Cultural appreciation for diverse populations conceivably supports biracial identification. Geographic region has an even stronger impact on the dependent variable. Southern Blacks are over 40 percent less likely than Blacks in other regions to report biracial identification with Whites.

Analysis Summary

Extending Peter Blau's conceptualization of intergroup relations to interracial identification supports using biracial identification as a social distance indicator and also contributes to the collective understanding of the racial identification process. Indeed, 91.1 percent of the geographical variation in Black biracial identification with Whites is attributable to exposure to Whites, educational equality with Whites, Black group size relative to Whites, foreign-born Black representation, and geographic region. The more Black social circles intersect with that of Whites, the more Blacks report biracial identification with Whites. But with monoracial Black identification the default, greater equality and larger Black group sizes decrease the likelihood Blacks break old social norms and report biracial identification. This is because a larger availability of same-status, shared-race others naturally breeds in-group allegiance. Overall, the R^2 for this multivariate model, coupled with statistically significant results for all major postulates in the hypothesized directions, provides significant support for Blau's macrostructural theory.

DISCUSSION ON BLACK-WHITE
BIRACIAL INCIDENCE FINDINGS

This study borrows from Peter Blau's macrostructural theory on intergroup relations and subsequent empirical scholarship on interracial marriage to assess the effects of macrostructural variables on the likelihood of Black Americans reporting biracial identification with Whites. I evaluate the extent social forces known to influence interracial marriage also influence interracial identification, but the objective of this work is not just about theoretical extension. Rather, it is to build upon the body of knowledge and the social policies aimed at racial integration in America.

The application of interracial marriage as a means of measuring structural influence on racial integration depends on assumptions about marriage that are not as valid today as they once were. Because of widespread cohabitation, partnerships not legally recognized as marriage, divorce, and non-marital childbearing, one purpose of this book is to seize the opportunity to utilize newly established data on biracial *people*, rather than biracial *marriage*, and establish the former as an improved social indicator of interracial relations. Conditions under which Blau's theory can be extended from interracial marriage to interracial people are confirmed here. And the explanatory power of the model surpasses similar studies using biracial marriage as an indicator of racial integration.

This chapter demonstrates that structural parameters theoretically and empirically known to increase biracial marriage also increase biracial offspring, or at least the liberty and motive to identify as such. Whether greater biracial identification signifies greater biracial progeny, or simply a greater freedom to express biracial heritage, remains unknown (Harris 2002). The new race question format, which made its debut on the 2000 U.S. Census, echoes the dynamic nature of race as an internalized choice reflecting external perceptions and conditions (Brown, Hitlin and Elder 2007; Hirschman et al. 2000; Hitlin, Brown and Elder 2007). As illustrated in this chapter, macrostructural parameters have the power to accommodate or constrain this choice. Certainly, other factors such as age, gender, networks, family structure, parent-gender/race nexus, and political temperament affect both identity and identification. Additionally, racial identification changes over time, place, and context (Brown et al. 2007; Saperstein 2006). However, the boundaries defining microsocial and macrostructural forces are blurred in the midst of implicitly contemplating identity and explicitly reporting identification, and no robust empirical approach to date has effectively captured this fluidity (Harris 2002).

With such a socially constructed process perpetually in flux, self-identification is perhaps the only plausible race measure in contemporary society.
Although identification may be developed within immediate social contexts,
with cultural influences configuring the degree structural features constrain
the choice, the environments where those social networks exist are governed
by a macrostructural juggernaut. In fact, Blau repeatedly infers that social
structure trumps cultural mediators. Furthermore, consistent empiricism
supports the overriding effects of exposure, inequality, and group size over
cultural influences on interracial relations (Anderson and Saenz 1994; Blum
1985; Fitzpatrick and Hwang 1992; Rytina et al. 1988). Conclusively, theory
and empiricism agree that cultural effects on biracial identification wax and
wane to the degree structural forces permit.

It is difficult to conclude whether greater interracial contact results in
greater rejection of one or both races, greater identification with one or both
races, or simply more interracial intimacy—each increasing biracial identification prevalence. The thinking in this book assumes biracial identification
embraces, rather than rejects, both races—thereby indicating a closing gap in
social distance. This highlights a notable feedback loop guiding Blau's work.
As the minority group size increases, majority group discrimination also
increases and the gap between the percent of Blacks who marry Whites, and
the percent of Whites who marry Blacks, narrows. As discrimination toward
the racial minority increases, the discrepancy between those claiming a
Black-White biracial identification as a percentage of total Blacks, and those
claiming a Black-White biracial identification as a percentage of total Whites
also closes. More biracial individuals identify as single-race Black due to
oppositional responses to discrimination, as well as White treatment and
perception projections onto the self. Both are bound to intensify as Whites
are increasingly exposed to a growing Black minority. At the same time,
Blacks have less exposure to Whites due to self-sustaining community size,
increased discrimination, White-flight, and so on. In this way, it becomes
understandable how relative group prevalence can affect (and be affected by)
residential exposure, racial equality, and minority group size, as moderated
by varying degrees of discrimination. These factors reciprocally influence
the social distance between Blacks and Whites exemplified by the choice
for biracial identification. Some scholars have suggested that most Blacks in
America are of mixed-race (Davis 1991; Lee and Bean 2004; Spencer 1997);
therefore, recognizing and understanding how structural parameters influence biracial identification over time will be of cultural and macrostructural
import.

Increasing profusion of biracial unions and offspring interactively decreases
racial salience and encourages biracial identification. This relationship

between prevalence and possibility makes speculation on the direction of causation impossible. However, using biracial identification to evaluate the degree structural features impact racial distance is the purpose of this work. Investigating the structural parameters influencing choices to break hypo-descent norms allows for a better understanding, albeit indirectly, of macro-social constraints rejecting partial White heritage.

Blau's work effectively hypothesizes that Black penetration into White society increases interracial marriage; however, the latter is more than just a numerical product of the former. When degree is intimate and temper is affable, "high rates of intermarriage are considered to be indicative of social integration because they reveal intimate and profound relations between members of different groups and strata are—more or less—socially accept-able" (Blau et al. 1984:591). Blau stresses interracial marriage is more likely for minorities due to demographic consolidation (i.e., the extent race is correlated with several other characteristics at once), inequality, and group size. Furthermore, the greater the discrepancy between racial minority and majority proportions, the greater the gap between each group's interracial marriage incidence because such intimacies encounter more resistance by the larger group when such occurrences are less prevalent. Exogamy and bira-cial identification are not interpreted here as Black assimilation into White society, but rather a mutual endorsement of imploding structural and cultural boundaries synergistically enhancing mobility and diversity to the benefit of our societal fabric.

Many empirical studies have tested various aspects of Blau's theory on interracial relations. However, no previous study has applied work on biracial marriage to biracial identification (with the exception of my published pilot study in 2008). By extending Blau's intersection-interaction-intermarriage-interdependence link to also include "interracial identification," the analysis detailed in this chapter demonstrates advantages of employing biracial iden-tification as a precise social distance indicator between Blacks and Whites.

Presumably, biracial identification prevalence is both the result of inter-racial unions and a willingness to report recent multiracial heritage (Lee and Bean 2007b; Perlmann and Waters 2002). As mentioned, other studies find biracial Blacks to be the least likely biracial group to report biracial iden-tification. Although boundaries for membership in the White race appear to be shifting in some areas, those with recent Black heritage continue to be socially restrained from participating in this phenomenon—despite their eligibility to do so (Loveman and Muniz 2007). Whereas biracial individuals identifying as such demonstrate some degree of boundary-crossing, Black-White biracial individuals may be more restricted from partaking in this type of mobility than other biracial individuals because social and structural constraints continue to prohibit Blacks from transcending Black categorization. These trends potentially sustain the increasing assertions that a Black/non-Black dichotomy best describes the state of race in the United States (Brunsma 2005; Fischer 2003; Gans 2007; Hochschild and Weaver 2007; Lee and Bean 2007a). Whereas some racial groups have been able to pierce, or at least budge symbolic racial boundaries, biracial Black mobility continues to be retarded by macrostructural and cultural influences.

In closing, this chapter sets out asking which factors influence biracial identification. This question has been asked and answered by many before me. Decades of qualitative research has identified highly personal and social psychological factors influencing one's racial identity. This work has informed important racial identity frameworks used by other scholars deploying quantitative methods to confirm and build upon the body of knowledge in this discipline. Gathering large-scale data on biracial populations was a challenge before the 2000 Census. A recent surge of quantitative work takes advantage of this groundbreaking data source to assess the influence of personal and familial demographics, social network compositions, and other meso-level factors on racial identification at both the individual and the group levels. Although many of these have peppered in macro-level factors such as segregation and group size, what has been missing is a macrostructural perspective asking why some cities have greater biracial identification incidence than others.

This chapter aimed to fill this gap by answering that very question. Not only is racial identification influenced by micro- and meso-level factors, I find that it is also influenced by macro-level factors. We know from previous research that racial identity and identification is influenced by personal social psychological factors, personal sociodemographic factors, and immediate social setting/social network factors. Now we know that racial identification is also influenced by the broader urban composition. To review, a city's segregation intensity influences biracial identification incidence in that city. How evenly higher education attainment is distributed across racial groups in a city also influences biracial identification incidence in that city. The racial composition and nativity incidence of a city influences its biracial identification incidence. And the geographic region in which a city sits also influences the likelihood that the people living in it will identify biracially.

Racial identification is a choice. This chapter adds new factors to the list of dynamics influencing that choice by addressing why Black biracial identification incidence with Whites is high in some cities and low in others. Now the question becomes whether different groups are affected differently by the same factors. Blau does not stipulate how his theory might affect different racial groups differently because his theory examines the dynamics affecting intergroup relations in general (and these could be on the basis of religion, social class, race, etc.). It is largely empiricists testing his theory, including Blau himself at times, who use "race" to define one's group. These studies investigate relationships between Blacks and Whites, Asians and Whites, or Hispanics and Whites. The next chapter in this book repeats the analysis just performed (on Black biracial identification incidence with Whites) on Asian biracial identification incidence with Whites. The first purpose is to confirm support of extending the macrostructural theory of intergroup relations to the adjacent context of intergroup identification, as theoretical extension would not be in order if the explanatory power was limited to only one segment of the population. The second purpose, albeit perhaps more primary, is to be able to answer the question of why different groups are affected by the same things differently. I argue that a study of race relations is not complete with it, as we cannot understand the magnitude of one group's situation without using comparison groups to capture and quantify relativity.

NOTE

1. As a dummy variable, region cannot be transformed because ln(0) is undefined.

Chapter 3

Structural Influence on Asian Biracial Identification with Whites

The 2000 U.S. Census allowed respondents to describe themselves with more than one racial category for the first time in census history. Nearly 7 million individuals took advantage of this freedom, and this figure grew by 32.0 percent (to 9 million) by 2010, despite a total American population increase of only 9.7 percent. That is, the biracial population count grew more than three times as much as the total population in the years 2000–2010. But the trends differ by race.

Among 17.3 million Asian Americans in 2010, 1.6 million identified as half White. About the same number of Blacks identified as half White (1.8 million), despite the fact that Blacks are nearly two and a half times the size of Asians in the United States. Why are Asians more than twice as likely as Blacks to choose to biracially identify with Whites?

Let's compare the two groups another way. The ratio of Asians to Whites is 0.08. If race had no meaning whatsoever, one would expect the biracial Asian-White population to be about 8 percent. That's not actually too far off; the Asian-White biracial incidence is as high as 9.4 percent. But it is interesting that the actual incidence is greater than what chance would expect, given that we see the opposite relationship in Blacks. The ratio of Blacks to Whites is 0.18. As such, chance would expect the biracial Black-White population to be about 18 percent, yet Black-White biracial incidence is as low as 4.4 percent. Put this way, the difference in the relationship between each of the two racial minority groups and Whites is even more striking. Responses to the census race question confirm racial identification is a choice (Harris and Sim 2002; Hirschman 2004; Masuoka 2011). But which factors influence that choice and why?

Much has been done over the decades to qualitatively understand which personal factors influence racial categorization. Such work tends to focus on the role of racial identity (rather than racial identification), which is based on one's self-understanding through lived experience (Rockquemore and Brunsma 2008). As an internalized process perpetually in flux, it may not always or exactly match forced-choice classifications on institutional forms (Hirschman, Alba and Farley 2000; Hitlin, Brown and Elder 2006; Saperstein 2006). Most scholars find that racial identity and racial identification are closely aligned however.

Empiricists depend on racial identification (rather than racial identity) when research relies on the quantitative analysis of a significant sample size across multiple racial groups and geographies (Brown, Hitlin and Elder 2006; Renn 2008). However, much less work has been done to quantitatively understand what influences racial identification at scale because the availability of the data was limited before the 2000 Census. Quantitative racial identification studies focus on individual-level (and sometimes household- or group-level) units of analysis. They operate in the micro-level and meso-level setting. That is, how one's age or education (or that of their parents) influences their racial identification. Such a line of inquiry is extremely important to unpacking the sociodemographic and socio-psychological factors influencing the racial understanding of one's self, which is in large part a reflection of our racial understanding of society. Between qualitative work over the decades and quantitative work in more recent years, the study of individual- and household-level racial identification has been well-researched.

What's missing (until now) is large-scale, quantitative inquiry into the macro-level factors influencing the racial identification of groups. Such an analysis would focus on city-level units of analysis, as macrostructural factors vary geographically. Not coincidently, so do biracial identification incidences. Indeed, there is considerable geographic variation in the proportion of racial minorities that identify as biracial (Farley 2002; Hoeffel et al. 2012). Drastic variation in the 2010 Census ranges from 4.5 percent in New York City to 35.4 percent in Coeur d'Alene among biracial Asians identified as half White. Greater biracial populations skew toward areas where racial minorities represent a relatively small proportion of the population (Butts 2008). This and other distinctions across metropolitan areas hint at underlying structural differences affecting the likelihood of biracial identification.

Although macrostructural work to understand biracial identification incidence is new, macrostructural work to understand biracial marriage incidence is not. Borrowing from prior theoretical and empirical scholarship on intergroup relations, this chapter explores how urban structural factors affecting biracial marriage impact the likelihood Asians report biracial identification with Whites across 363 metropolitan areas in the continental United States.

STRUCTURAL FACTORS AFFECTING ASIAN
RELATIONSHIPS WITH WHITES

Intergroup relations are often investigated through the lens of exchange (Fu and Heaton 2000; Kalmijn 1998; Lichter and Qian 2005; Qian 1997, 1999; Sassler and Joyner 2011), assimilation (Hwang, Saenz and Aguirre 1994; Kalmijn 1998; Qian 1999; Qian, Glick and Batson 2012), or opportunity-structure perspectives (Heaton and Jacobson 2000; Hwang et al. 1994; Kalmijn 1998; Kalmijn and Van Tubergen 2010; Qian 1999; Tucker and Mitchell-Kernan 1990). Peter Blau's macrostructural theory develops the opportunity-structure perspective (Blau 1977, 1994). This perspective rests on Simmel's (1908) notion of over-lapping social circles in which each social circle is based on a demographic (or lifestyle) characteristic. The characteristic that is most salient is the social circle in which the person feels the most belonging and therefore becomes their core identity group. People generally prefer to interact with members of their own core group; however, meaningful social relationships can happen between people from different groups if they are similar in many other ways. If these other social circles significantly intersect, shared commonalities become the grounds on which social relationships can be formed (despite belonging to different core groups).

Continuing to use the example of intermarriage as a form of intergroup relations, Blau adds to Simmel's concept by asserting that various structural factors help or hinder opportunities to satisfy one's desire to marry within one's group, making marrying-out more likely under certain conditions and less likely under others. Blau assumes the probability of marrying-in or out depends on a few key factors. First, he agrees with Simmel that the number of characteristics in common between members of two different groups affects the likelihood of relationship development. The more characteristics in common, the less the one unshared characteristic matters. But he adds to Simmel by arguing that this is a function of exposure—spatial opportunities for contact. Second, the numerical availability of same-race suitors that share other characteristics besides race affects the likelihood of marrying-in. When there are less same-race individuals of similar status on other characteristics like education or religious beliefs for example, there are proportionately more different-race individuals that share these statuses.

A third element, group size, plays a role within each of these two key factors. Rapidly growing minority groups tend to be geographically and socially segregated (Blalock 1967; Castles and Miller 2003; Massey and Denton 1993; Waters 1999; Wilson 1980). These groups become homogenous and delineated, limiting contact and the extent any characteristics are shared with the out-group (Blau 1980; Castles and Miller 2003; Qian et al. 2012; Sassen 2001, 2006; Waters 1999). At the same time, equality creates conditions that provide adequately sized in-group relationship opportunities with members of similar status—unless the minority group is small. In both cases, the theory maintains that same-race marriage will be more likely among members of large racial groups, while interracial marriage is more likely among members of small racial groups.

Blau's macrostructural theory of intergroup relations allows most any demographic variable to be used to define and delineate groups (e.g., religion, class, age). In the twenty-first-century United States, the theory clearly lends itself to race as a salient characteristic still defining in-group and out-group today. However groups are defined, Blau's theory can conceivably explain any type of relation between members of different groups (e.g., marriage, cohabitation, friendship). The theory has been used to explain the probability of several different types of interracial relations, including interracial contact, conflict, and marriage. Marriage has always been the most popular among these. Postulates explaining differences in interracial marriage incidence across geographies include those centered on demographic consolidation (i.e., the extent race is correlated with several other characteristics at once), inequality, and group size.

Demographic Consolidation among Asians

The theory asserts that relations can happen between members of different races if most of their other social circles intersect. Race, however, tends to have correlations with many other characteristics, thereby inhibiting the chances that members of two racial groups share the social circles on which relationships are formed. Heightened racial salience, intolerance of dissimilar others, and antagonistic allegiance in opposition to institutional and interpersonal racism have a way of consolidating sociodemographic characteristics and homogenizing the minority group (Blau 1980; Castles and Miller 2003; Qian et al. 2012; Sassen 2001, 2006; Waters 1999). These should not be new concepts for most readers thinking about Blacks in America. But some readers may be less aware of circumstances like these faced by Asians in certain parts of the country. Interracial relations are theorized to be less likely here— not just for Blacks but for Asians as well because social circles for members of different racial groups do not intersect under these conditions.

Residential segregation best operationalizes this concept (Anderson and Saenz 1994; Kalmijn 1998; Kalmijn and Van Tubergen 2010). Segregation limits the number of similarities between racial groups. Such geographical confinement creates cultural and social barriers by consolidating characteristics that would otherwise vary (e.g., employment opportunities, healthcare access, and religious denomination attendance). That is, residential segregation has a way of completely segregating racial groups in a multitude of ways beyond simply separating domiciles (Massey and Denton 1993; Qian et al. 2012).

The effect is especially compounded in cities where the racial minority group is quite large. When an oppressed racial group is large, the majority racial group perceives threat and responds with behaviors and actions that serve to keep the large minority group separated, both geographically and socially (Blalock 1967; Massey and Denton 1993; Waters 1999; Wilson 1980). In the United States, very large Asian populations exist in New York and Los Angeles where Asians are quite segregated from Whites.

When segregation limits minority social operations to immediate neighborhoods, quality contact with the majority group is rare (Fitzpatrick and Hwang 1992). Without regular opportunities for contact, commonalities, or interpersonal respect, interracial relations are arguably less likely (Blau 1994). But when race is less correlated with the distribution of other sociodemographic characteristics, the racial minority group is more exposed to the majority group on common ground and interracial relations are consistently found to be more likely (Anderson and Saenz 1994; Blau 1994; Blau, Beeker and Fitzpatrick 1984; Blau and Schwartz 1984; Blum 1984, 1985; Fitzpatrick and Hwang 1992; Heaton and Jacobson 2000; Lichter 2013; Qian 1999; Qian et al. 2012; Skvoretz 1990).

Race itself doesn't hinder interracial relations; it is the geographical and structural boundaries people create that do (Park and Burgess 1921). Indeed, Zubrinsky and Bobo (1996) find Asian segregation caused by racial discrimination, not by income differences or balkanization. *Balkanization* is a kind of self-segregation based on a preference for similar others and is often seen in school cafeterias today when the jocks sit at one table and the drama club kids sit at another. Another example of balkanization is the ethnic enclave, where newer immigrant groups residentially and commercially cluster in order to leverage their own network addressing their own specific needs before (or in place of) assimilating into the broader society. Although it could be argued that balkanization is in fact part of a feedback loop in which some inclusion/exclusion behaviors by the ruling-class group are in fact imposed on the oppressed group, segregation proper is largely involuntary to be sure.

Segregation tends to be more common among large minority groups (Park and Burgess 1921) or racial minority groups with recent and active immigration flow (Castles and Miller 2003). Asians are not a large racial minority group, but they are the fastest growing racial group in the United States[1] due to recent and active immigration flows (Edmonston, Lee and Passel 2002; Hoeffel et al. 2012). Although less common and less severe than residential segregation endured by Blacks, which is declining over time, Asians are indeed segregated in some cities, where there have been no recent declines (Farley 2011; Zubrinsky and Bobo 1996). The theory argues that decreasing exposure between races decreases the likelihood of interracial marriage, but results from empiricism on whether this is true for Asians has been mixed. Whereas Qian et al. (2012) find that Asian residential segregation reduces Asian interracial marriage, Hwang et al. (1994) yield inconclusive results. Empiricists do agree, however, that Asians have more interracial contact with Whites, less social distance from Whites, and therefore are more likely to interracially marry than Blacks (Brunsma 2007; Masuoka 2011; Roth 2005).

Inequality between Asians and Whites

The theory assumes people prefer to interact with members of their own racial group, so long as they are similar in most other ways (Blau 1977; Simmel 1908; see also Kalmijn and Van Tubergen 2010). However, Blau's contribution rests on the premise that there are certain conditions limiting the availability of same-race associates who also share other characteristics. The likelihood of interracial relations is increased when the proportion of same-status, different-race options is larger than the proportion of same-status, same-race suitors.

The effect of one's status, or station in life, is often operationalized through (in)equality measurements because relationships depend on commonalities forged on the basis of equality (Blau 1977; Lichter 2013; Zhang and Vanhook 2009). Blau (1977) defines inequality as the relative difference between two groups on an interval-measured variable, such as education. Rytina et al. (1988) statistically confirm that education is the most suitable inequality measure for use in this theory, arguing the volatility of income cannot compete with the more stable status associated with education.

The relative difference between racial groups on educational attainment affects interracial relations in different ways. On the one hand, as more minorities have access to higher education, the salience of race is reduced (Blau 1977, 1994; Broman, Neighbors and Jackson 1998; Croll 2007; Kalmijn 1993; Qian et al. 2012). Shared non-race characteristics and interests become more interpersonally relevant, making interracial relationships more likely (Blum 1984; Fu and Heaton 2000; Gans 2007; Harris 2002; Heaton and Jacobson 2000; Kalmijn 1993; Kalmijn and Van Tubergen 2010; Lichter 2013; McPherson et al. 2001; Qian 1997, 1999) and more sustainable (Zhang and Vanhook 2009). On the other hand, increased upward mobility puts greater proportions of minorities in higher rung positions and, assuming the racial minority group size is adequate, increases the pool of same-status, same-race suitors (Blau 1977, 1994). As such, decreasing racial inequality at the macro-level decreases the likelihood of interracial relations despite decreased social distance at the more interpersonal level (Blau 1994; Blau et al. 1984; Blau et al. 1982; Rytina et al. 1988). This paradox is a function of group size, therefore relative group size must be considered alongside inequality in macro-level models such as this.

Group Size of Asians, Relative to Whites

The theory concludes that interracial relations are more likely among members of groups that are numerically small relative to the majority group. This is because numerically limited in-group options make out-group options statistically more probable. The effect is particularly apparent in race applications because smaller racial groups tend to be more heterogeneous and therefore are more distributed across various social dimensions where their social circles are likely to overlap with the majority group.

Because smaller racial groups are more likely to share multiple non-race characteristics, interests, and activities in common venues with members of other racial groups, interracial relations are more likely (Blau 1977, 1994; Blau and Schwartz 1984; Frey and Farley 1996; Fu and Heaton 2000; Heaton and Jacobson 2000; Hwang et al. 1994; Kalmijn and Van Tubergen 2010; Qian 1999). Furthermore, minorities from smaller racial groups who break away from the norm for their group are more likely to intermarry because the selection pool of same-status, same-race suitors is numerically limited (Blau 1994; Heaton and Jacobson 2000; Kalmijn 1998; Kalmijn and Van Tubergen 2010; Qian et al. 2012; St. John and Clymer 2000). That is, small groups are an exception to the uniquely macro-level phenomenon where increasing equality decreases interracial relations. Again, at micro- and meso-levels of analysis, greater educational equality tends to facilitate interracial marriage, but at macro-level, group size interferes and paradoxically turns the relationship around.

Structural factors such as demographic consolidation, inequality, and group size have repeatedly been shown to affect the likelihood of relations with different-race others. Most tests of Blau's theory have focused on interracial marriage, in part due to the availability of large-scale, quantitative data of sufficient sample size (Blau 1994), and in part due to the argument that "marriage is undoubtedly the most profound and lasting human relation of all those voluntarily established" (Blau et al. 1984:591). This implies interracial marriage is more suitable than other forms of interracial contact for observing structural influences on racial integration because of its durability and longevity.

Contemporary American society, however, is characterized by widespread cohabitation, partnerships not legally recognized as marriage, divorce, and non-marital childbearing. Interracial couples are more likely to cohabitate than marry (Kalmijn 1993; Lichter and Qian 2005; Qian et al. 2012), more likely to divorce (Zhang and Van Hook 2009), and more likely to produce children out of wedlock (Kalmijn 1993), than same-race couples. Although intermarriage incidence has commonly been used to indicate social distance (Fu and Heaton 2000; Kalmijn 1998; Kalmijn and Van Tubergen 2010; Lee and Bean 2004; Lichter and Qian 2005; Qian et al. 2012; Suro 1999; Zhang and Vanhook 2009), its footing as a preferred racial integration indicator is becoming less steady (Brunsma 2005).

Biracial marriage incidence and biracial identification incidence are both indicative of social distance between races (Bean and Stevens 2003; Bratter 2007; Butts 2008, 2009; Fu and Heaton 2000; Kalmijn 1998; Kalmijn and Van Tubergen 2010; Lee and Bean 2004; Lichter and Qian 2005; Qian et al. 2012; Suro 1999; Zhang and Vanhook 2009). However, biracial identification is potentially a more salient indicator of integration than biracial marriage in today's society (Butts 2008; Kalmijn 1993). The flexibility of the new census race question more accurately tallies variations in racial groups than ever before. This gives demographers the opportunity to leverage data on biracial *people*, rather than data on biracial *marriage*, as an emerging social distance indicator (Bean and Stevens 2003; Bratter 2007; Lee and Bean 2004).

FACTORS AFFECTING ASIAN-WHITE INTERRACIAL IDENTIFICATION

Mixed-race identity, identification processes, and experiences have been a common line of sociological inquiry for many years. These studies come largely in the form of qualitative, micro-level studies of individuals and quantitative, micro- and/or meso-level analyses examining the influence of families, social networks, and immediate neighborhoods on an individual's racial identity or racial identification. In recent years, considerable quantitative advancements have been made in understanding various determinants of multiracial identification. These studies generally examine the influence of sociodemographic and social psychological factors on racial identification, but still focus on individuals, households, and sometimes groups as the unit of analysis.

Although they focus on micro-level characteristics and meso-level contexts, as opposed a macro-level view, they do offer findings that will help to inform my hypotheses in the next section, particularly studies that test exposure to other racial groups, education, group size, nativity, and region. Several studies agree that the racial diversity of one's neighborhood influences whether one chooses monoracial or multiracial identification, with individuals living in more diverse neighborhoods more likely to identify with more than one race (Bratter 2007; Croll 2007; Harris 2002; Masuoka 2011;

Tafoya et al. 2005). The effect of educational attainment on whether one identifies multiracially is less clear. Some studies find that one's educational attainment generally encourages one to identify multiracially (Brunsma 2005; Croll 2007; Masuoka 2011; Roth 2005; Tafoya et al. 2005). Others find the opposite is true. With more education, Asians are more likely to identify as Asian alone (Bratter 2007; Hochschild and Weaver 2007; Roth 2005). The effect of group size on multiracial identification is more consistent. Xie and Goyette (1997) find that as the local Asian group size increases, the likelihood of multiracial Asians identifying as monoracial Asian increases. Harris and Sim (2002) find that as the local White group size increases, the likelihood of multiracial Asians identifying as monoracial White increases. Immigrants are less likely to identify multiracially (Bean and Stevens 2003; Masuoka 2011; Roth 2005; Tafoya et al. 2005). And, of course, trends vary by region (Bean and Stevens 2003; Croll 2007; Harris and Sim 2002; Masuoka 2011; Rockquemore and Brunsma 2008; Roth 2005). Overall, these studies are generally and directionally consistent with my findings examining macro-structural influence on biracial Black identification described in the previous chapter and lend support for what might be expected of a comparable analysis of Asian biracial identification later in this chapter.

Census 2000 presents an exciting opportunity to extend empirical work on Asian-White biracial populations to macro-level perspectives. Nearly as many Asians as Blacks identified as half White on the 2010 census (1.6 million and 1.8 million, respectively) despite the fact that the total Asian American population is 2.4 times smaller in number than the total Black population. Given the ratio of Blacks to Whites, chance would expect as many as 18.2 percent of the total Black population to be half White, yet only 4.4 percent of the Black population identified as such. But given the ratio of Asians to Whites, chance would expect only 7.5 percent of the total Asian American population to be half White, yet as many as 9.4 percent identified as such. In other words, Blacks identify as half White 75 percent *less* than would be expected due to chance, while Asians identify as half White 25 percent *more* than would be expected.

Before we can understand the macrostructural dynamics influencing biracial identification incidence, we must dive into this delta. This is much easier said than done, as many would argue (including me) that the histories behind the experiences of Blacks and Asian Americans simply can't be compared. But knowing that biracial identification today is affected by long and tumultuous racial group histories, and the consequences of those histories on the current racial climate, an overview is in order.

To begin, the racial identification process is different for Asians who are half White than for Blacks who are half White (Lou, Lalonde and Wilson 2011; Roth 2005; Wilton, Sanchez and Garcia 2013). As discussed previously, Blacks are subjected to hypodescents. These clear and established social norms pressure individuals with partial Black heritage to default to a monoracial Black identity (and presumably, by extension, to racial identification). Meanwhile, these social norms do not necessarily influence Asian American racial identity. In fact, racial identification studies of biracial Asian children find that the parents are more likely to identify their kids as White than they are to identify them as Asian when only one racial category is allowed (Roth 2005; Xie and Goyette 1997). Even once the multiracial option became available in 2000 and many such children were identified as both Asian and White, those whose parents chose to continue to identify them monoracially were still more likely to indicate "White" as the race of their child than to indicate "Asian" (Roth 2005). Overall, these kinds of studies suggest that biracial Asians have considerably more flexibility in racial classification choices than Blacks.

Meanwhile, several studies find that residential segregation and racial discrimination discourage multiracial identification (Brunsma 2005; Harris 2002; Hochschild and Weaver 2007; Masuoka 2011; Tafoya 2002; Tafoya et al. 2005). Asians do have the greatest rates of homeownership, median income, marriage stability, educational attainment, and what I'll call *interneighboring* with Whites than any other racial minority (Xie and Goyette 2004; Zhang and Vanhook 2009; Zubrinsky and Bobo 1996). As such, I would expect this to help explain differences in the prevalence of Asian and Black biracial identification with Whites.

Residential segregation, a form of racial discrimination, is a symptom of chronic racism. Although it is argued that Asians experience more racism, prejudice, and discrimination in the United States than is commonly acknowledged (Alvarez, Juang and Liang 2006; JACL 2008; Song 2003), the history of racism between Whites and Blacks and Asians, and the present-day consequences of those histories, cannot be directly compared. Whereas Blacks have endured involuntary immigration, centuries of slavery, oppression reproduced over generations, more intense and widespread segregation and denial of identity validation by hypodescent standards, Asians have been subjected to internment camps, property seizures, patriotic loyalty and citizenship interrogation, mainstream media ridicule, and a more recent history of overt anti-racial group legislation (Lou, Lalonde and Wilson 2011; Song 2003). Compared to Blacks, today's Asians face more employment discrimination and issues voting, and lack political representation, despite the guise of the "model minority" myth (JACL 2008). Meanwhile, Blacks are nearly seventeen times as likely as Asians to be killed by police (Mapping Police Violence 2020). It's clear the two groups have experienced completely different modes and magnitudes of racism, and I would expect this to help explain differences in the prevalence of biracial identification with Whites.

Now let's look at racial discrimination. The wage gap for Asians is unique; dollar for dollar, Asians make more money for comparable work than similarly qualified, same-gender Whites. Asian women make four cents on the dollar more than White women, and Black women make one cent less than White women. Asian men make two cents more than White men, and Black men make two cents less than White men. Therefore, the wage gap between Asians and Blacks is 4–5 percent (PayScale 2020). In a dual income household with a man and a woman, Asian families make 9 percent more for the same work as similarly qualified Black families. This is a considerable advantage for Asians, especially when one considers the summed income advantage over the career span.

Wage gaps look at similarly qualified workers in similar jobs. But the reality of the situation is that the Asian advantage goes beyond that. Blacks are not proportionately represented in the same job categories held by Asians. Whereas wage gap metrics would estimate Black households to make about 9 percent less than Asian households, the reality is that real median household income among Blacks is more than 50 percent less than that of Asians. That is, Asian families make more than twice the income *annually* (about $81K) as Black families (about $40K), with White families making around $68K for comparison (U.S. Census Bureau 2018). Now consider the summed income advantage of Asians to Blacks over the career span.

Some scholars argue that the Asian advantage (over Whites) elicits jealousy and fuels hatred. "Indeed, the perception of Asian Americans as 'foreigners' who present an economic, educational, or cultural threat may elicit racial dynamics that are quite distinct from the experiences of African Americans" (Alvarez et al. 2006:478). The psychology of the ruling class struggles to admit to jealousy of a minority group, however, so it searches for other reasons to justify its disdain (Arendt 1964; Blalock 1967). Asian Americans have been blamed and publicly shamed for illogical presumptions that, by association, they present a threat to American public health and safety after various infectious diseases originated in Asian countries. Examples include global, deadly epidemics such as the Asian Flu (1956), Hong Kong Flu (1968), SARS (2002), various bird flus such as H5N1 (1997, 2012, 2013), and most recently, COVID-19 (2019). Labels (e.g., "Chinese Virus") have been introduced into public discourse by prominent public officials and have coincided with a surge of physical assaults on Asian Americans in public settings. Similar experiences have been common over the past century, whether the association of Asians was with a pandemic, a world war, or with despised forms of government such as communism. If Asians have experienced hate crimes based simply on "how they look," I imagine cities with greater division between Asians and Whites will have less Asian-White biracial identification incidence. Given these high-stake implications, analyzing differences in structural influence on each of these groups seems more important than ever.

HYPOTHESIZING THE INFLUENCE OF STRUCTURE ON ASIAN BIRACIAL IDENTIFICATION WITH WHITES

This study applies concepts drawn from Blau's macrostructural theory on biracial marriage to understand how structural factors affect Asian-White biracial identification differently than Black-White biracial identification as tested in the previous chapter. The theory assumes that smaller groups experience less discrimination and inequality, and proposes two key postulates. First, cities with less discrimination are more likely to be conducive to opportunities for healthy interracial exposure. Second, cities with less inequality increase social mobility for racial minorities. This decreases racial salience and helps to close the social distance gap between racial groups. However, increased upward mobility does put greater proportions of racial minorities in higher rung positions and, assuming adequate group size, actually increases the pool of same-status, same-race marriage partner options. These dynamics facilitate healthy interracial exposure but actually serve to increase the likelihood of same-race relationships.

Factors facilitating interracial marriage may also encourage interracial identification. This feedback loop supports testing the aptness of biracial identification in demonstrating the effect of structural parameters on social distances between racial groups. It is hypothesized that the same parameters influencing Asian-White interracial marriage also influence Asian-White interracial identification. Hence,

H_1. The more social circles between Asians and Whites intersect, the greater the likelihood Asians will report biracial identification with Whites.

H_2. The greater the educational equality between Asians and Whites, the greater the likelihood Asians will report monoracial Asian identification.

H_3. The smaller the Asian group size relative to Whites, the greater the likelihood Asians will report biracial identification with Whites.

DATA AND METHODS

Social structure is embodied by multidimensional social arrangements between proximal groups of people (Blau 1994). Kalmijn and Van Tubergen (2010) recommend measuring social structure using geographical units more granular than the state-level. In the United States, diverse populations living in close proximity characterize urban centers (McPherson et al. 2001). Metropolitan areas have been the primary pallet for interracial contact since the antebellum period (Wilson 1980). With the availability of large-scale, quantitative data at this level of analysis, metropolitan areas including MSAs and metropolitan NECTAs are natural units for measuring interracial contact, and conceivably, interracial identification. There are 363 metropolitan areas in the continental United States. All are used in this analysis.

Dependent Variable: Asian-White Biracial Identification Incidence

For the first time in U.S. history, the 2000 Census allowed residents to mark more than one racial category and this policy was continued in 2010. The 2010 U.S. Census race question offers several categories: White; Black, African American, or Negro; American Indian or Alaska Native; Asian; Native Hawaiian and Other Pacific Islander; and Some Other Race. For each city, the percentage of all Asian Americans identifying as also White is calculated using data reported in Census Summary File 1. The data show that considerably more Asians claim biracial identification with Whites than the odds would predict; although the ratio of Asians to Whites is 0.08, as many as 9.4 percent of Asians claim biracial identification with Whites. Metropolitan areas range from 4.5 percent of Asians claiming Asian-White identification in New York City (where Asians represent 10.9 percent of the population) to 35.4 percent in Coeur d'Alene, Idaho (where Asians represent as little as 1.3 percent of the population).

Independent Variables: Structural Factors Affecting Asians and Whites

Several structural variables are hypothesized to explain the variance in biracial identification prevalence across geographies. These include interracial exposure (i.e., the opposite of the demographic consolidation characteristic of racial segregation), racial equality (i.e., the opposite of inequality), and Asian group size relative to Whites.

Asian Exposure to Whites

Racial segregation not only controls where people live, it also stifles the extent to which demographic and lifestyle characteristics are free to vary. In other words, the conditions of segregation result in a homogenization of other demographic characteristics. Specifically, people living in segregated neighborhoods not only share the same race but also largely share the same income bracket, educational achievement levels, likelihood to be gainfully employed, and so on, and are thenceforth likely to follow similar behavioral and life choice patterns, which then perpetuate the cycle. Coupled with geographic, cultural, and social delineation from the rest of society, these dynamics limit exposure to Whites. Inter-neighboring, on the other hand, introduces many opportunities for interracial interaction (Marsden 1990; Peach 1996; St. John and Clymer 2000), interracial marriage (Anderson and Saenz 1994; Blau et al. 1984; Blau and Schwartz 1984; Blum 1984, 1985; Fitzpatrick and Hwang 1992; Heaton and Jacobson 2000; Lichter 2013; Qian 1999; Qian et al. 2012), and biracial identification (Tafoya 2002; Xie and Goyette 1997).

Exposure of one racial group to another is measured by the exposure index (Population Studies Center 2013). This index measures the probability of interaction between one group and another by taking the average percentage of an area that is group-a, within the neighborhood (i.e., census tract) of a group-b person. Neighborhood compositions are listed for average White persons, Black persons, Asian persons, and Hispanic persons in the United States by the average percentage of each area that is White, Black, American Indian/Alaskan Native, Hawaiian/Pacific Islander, other race, two or more races, or Hispanic. The theoretical framework leveraged in this chapter is concerned with the relationship between a majority group and a minority group. In this case, I'm concerned with the exposure Asians have to Whites in order to see how this influences the percentage of Asians that biracially identify as also White. As such, I do not take the inverse (i.e., the average percentage of an area that is Asian, within the neighborhood of a White person). Rather, I take the index that measures the probability of interaction between Asians and Whites by taking the average percentage of an area that is White, within the neighborhood (i.e., census tract) of an Asian American person. The exposure index for each metropolitan area can theoretically range from 0 (indicating no exposure between Asians and Whites) to a number equal to the proportion of the population that is White in a city with only one Asian American. An exposure score calculated from 2010 census data for each metropolitan area is available from the University of Michigan Population Studies Center. Asian exposure to Whites ranges from 5.7 in Laredo, Texas, where Asians are segregated from Whites, to 95.4 in Altoona, Pennsylvania, where Asians are residentially integrated with Whites.

Racial Equality between Asians and Whites

Equality in college education has been shown to influence interracial marriage (Heaton and Jacobson 2000; Kalmijn 1998; Lichter 2013; Qian 1997, 1999; Qian et al. 2012) and is therefore expected to also influence biracial identification. For each metropolitan area in the 2007–2011 ACS, chi-square is calculated for the relationship between race and education by dividing the raw chi-square term by the maximum chi-square value (and then multiplying by 100). Because chi-square indicates the extent census frequencies deviate from what would be expected if race and education were independent, higher scores indicate greater deviation from independence between race and education, implying educational attainment is more dependent upon race. The calculated expression is subtracted from 100 to reverse the scale such that higher scores indicate greater educational parity (i.e., education is less dependent on race) between Asians and Whites. Scores range from 0.02 in Anderson, Indiana, where Asians and Whites are severely divided by education, to 5.35 in Columbus, Indiana, where Asians and Whites are more proportionately represented in each rung of an educational attainment hierarchy.

Asian Group Size Relative to Whites

Blau's theory assumes relative group size affects both exposure and equality (Blau 1977, 1994; Blau and Schwartz 1984). Most empirical tests of Blau's theory consider it a key theorem (Anderson and Saenz 1994; Butts 2008; Fitzpatrick and Hwang 1992; Heaton and Jacobson 2000; Qian 1999). Indeed, group size is often the strongest of all variables in tests evaluating structural determinants of interracial marriage (Kalmijn and Van Tubergen 2010). Relative group size is measured by the number of Asians per thousand single-race Whites. Data for this calculation is available from Census Summary File 1 for each metropolitan area. The ratio of Asians to 1,000 Whites ranges from 6.1 in Steubenville-Weirton, Ohio-West Virginia, where there are incredibly few Asians compared to Whites, to 711.8 in San Jose-Sunnyvale-Santa Clara, California, where there are a large number of Asians relative to Whites.

Control Variables

Other variables borrowed from Blau's theory and subsequent empirical tests isolate structural features. These include the percentage of the Asian population foreign-born and the geographic region in which the metro area is situated.

The percentage of the American Asian population that is foreign-born is controlled because areas with larger foreign-born populations tend to have more interracial marriage (Blau 1994; Lee and Bean 2004) and larger biracial populations (Bean and Stevens 2003; Lee and Bean 2004; Masuoka 2011; Roth 2005). The percentage of a racial group that is foreign-born affects the likelihood of interracial marriage and interracial progeny in part because immigrant presence can enhance diversity tolerance (Lee and Bean 2004). Though areas with greater Asian immigration incidence may indeed have greater interracial marriage incidence, the foreign-born Asians themselves are less likely to intermarry than their American-born counterparts

(Hwang et al. 1994; Lee and Fernandez 1998; Lichter and Qian 2005; Qian 1999). There are presumably some language barriers that would prove somewhat inhibitive. But also, those who immigrate in pursuit of higher education often arrive already married with focal families in tow (Castles and Miller 2003).

Largely, foreign-born racial minorities immigrate to the United States with different understandings of racial categories and what it means to be a racial minority than American-born minorities and second-generation immigrants of color (Masuoka 2011; Tafoya et al. 2005; Waters 1999). And just as immigrants are less likely to marry someone of another race, immigrants are also less likely to identify with more than one race (Bean and Stevens 2003; Masuoka 2011; Roth 2005; Tafoya et al. 2005). And because immigration is also related to inequality, a key parameter in macrostructural theory, it must be isolated (Blau 1977, 1994). Five-year estimates of the number of foreign-born Asians are available from the 2007–2011 ACS Table B16005, A-I. This measure is calculated as the percentage of total single-race Asians that are foreign-born, and ranges from 46.3 percent in Idaho Falls, Idaho, where more Asians were born in the United States, to 91.3 percent in Anderson, Indiana, where nearly all Asians were born outside the United States.

Similar to the way I expect immigrant presence to affect the central test variables in which I'm most interested (i.e., exposure, equality, and group size), I also expect geographic region to play a role just as it has in intermarriage studies. Regional variations reflect local culture. As such, geographic region does shape tolerance for interracial relations and whether race is or isn't the most defining demographic variable in choosing a spouse. Racial salience is more influential than other variables, especially on interracial relationship tolerance (Blum 1984; Heaton and Jacobson 2000; McPherson et al. 2001; Schwartz 1990). Regional variation effects on interaction can persist beyond the effects of exposure, equality, and group size due to racial identification strength, group allegiance, and solidarity (Brunsma 2005; Croll 2007; Hochschild and Weaver 2007).

I expect similar dynamics to affect interracial identification. Whereas I assigned the South as the comparison for Blacks in the last chapter, I assign the West as the comparison for Asians. The South is particularly distinguished for Blacks as compared to other regions around the United States in its means of production, politico-cultural institutions, and other contemporary ramifications of historical impact (Wilson 1980). The same might be said about Asians and the West, where a plurality of American Asians (44 percent) live. The average relative size of the Asian population in comparison to Whites across metropolitan areas in each region is greatest in the West. So it's not surprising given the earlier discussions in this book that Asian American discrimination is considered more intense in the West than in other regions (JACL 2008; Kitano et al. 1984). Here, Asians are more separated from Whites (as well as Blacks) compared to other areas in the United States.

Consistent with prior theory and empirical work, regions are coded into a dummy variable where the South, Midwest, and Northeast are coded as 1, and the West is coded as 0 to indicate the reference group. Given these conditions, one would expect that the percentage of Asians reporting biracial identification with Whites would be lowest in the West. But it is actually the highest. This trend anomaly may be due to other structural factors being tested in this analysis, presenting all the more support for controlling geographic region.

Analytic Design

OLS regression is used to analyze these data once natural log transformations are performed on all variables (except region[2]). Blau's final model (1994) logs all variables for four reasons. First, logging corrected nonlinearity and skewness to the right. Second, logging helped standardize the effects of different-sized metropolitan areas in the sample. Third, logging also standardized the different test variable scales in the model. Finally, logging circumvented the need for interaction terms. Once transformations were completed, these data meet regression assumptions. (Note that some multicollinearity is typical among structural parameters. Similar to prior studies, bivariate correlations between explanatory variables are high but do not violate multicollinearity tests.)

STRUCTURAL INFLUENCE ON ASIAN-WHITE BIRACIAL IDENTIFICATION

The average percentage (untransformed) of Asians reporting Asian-White biracial identification across 363 metropolitan areas is 15.4 percent, with 0.06 standard deviations. Bend, Oregon, and Coeur d'Alene, Idaho have percentages 3 standard deviations or greater (means of 33.0 percent or greater). Both cities are in the West where 19.4 percent of Asians claim Asian-White biracial identification. Nationally, 14.1 percent of Asians in the South, 13.2 percent in the Northeast, and 15.3 percent in the Midwest report biracial identification with Whites.

The correlation matrix and descriptive statistics for 363 metropolitan areas in the continental United States is shown in table 2.2. All explanatory variables correlate fairly strongly with the percentage of Asians reporting Asian-White biracial identification. This preliminarily supports the central research question, as macrostructural variables influencing biracial marriage seem to also influence biracial identification.

Bivariate Regression Analysis

The bivariate relationship between biracial identification incidence and each explanatory variable is displayed in table 2.3. Asian exposure to Whites explains 14.8 percent of the geographical variation in the percentage of Asians claiming Asian-White biracial identification, racial equality explains 30.3 percent, and Asian group size relative to Whites explains 29.8 percent. Consistent with interracial relations theory, Asian exposure to Whites is related to biracial identification in a positive direction; meaning, greater Asian exposure to Whites increases Asian biracial identification with Whites. Also as expected, greater educational equality between Asians and Whites decreases biracial identification. Lastly, group size is negatively related to biracial identification, just as the theory suggests. When the Asian group size is small, biracial identification prevalence is greater than when the Asian group size is large relative to Whites.

Both control variables are also statistically significant. Unlike the case with Blacks, the percentage of Asians foreign-born is negatively related to Asian biracial identification with Whites. That is, cities with greater proportions of Asians foreign-born tend to have less Asians identifying as half White. While Blacks in the focal region (i.e., the SouthBlack) are less likely to claim biracial identification as shown in the previous chapter, Asians in the focal region (i.e., the West) are actually more likely to claim Asian-White biracial identification.

Multiple Regression Analysis

The simultaneous regression of biracial identification on all the explanatory variables is shown in table 2.3. All variables significantly contribute to biracial identification incidence except the multivariate foreign-born coefficient. The full model accounts for 61.1 percent of the geographic variation in Asian biracial identification with Whites. That is, over 60 percent of geographic variation in the likelihood for Asians to identify as also White can be explained by the macrostructural variables included in this analysis.

The first hypothesis predicts that greater Asian exposure to Whites elicits greater Asian-White identification. Exposure strongly performs as expected, even with the effects of equality, group size, and control variables parsed away. A partial White heritage flourishes when Asians have more exposure to Whites; greater exposure may inspire greater identification with both groups, perhaps signifying less social distance between races. Conversely, when Asian exposure to Whites is limited, monoracial Asian identification is more prevalent, conceivably due to geographic, social, and cultural boundaries characteristic of segregated communities.

The second hypothesis predicts metropolitan areas with greater equality in education between Asians and Whites have fewer Asians reporting biracial identification with Whites. Equality is negatively related to biracial identification, though the effect is small. When Asians are proportionately represented in each educational attainment tier, same-race unions among Asians are more likely because of the availability of same-race, same-status suitors, and monoracial identification incidence follows suit.

The third hypothesis predicts that members of smaller Asian groups are more likely to identify as partly White. Consistent with biracial marriage studies where members of small racial minority groups are more likely to marry majority group members due to limited same-race options, biracial identification with Whites is more prevalent when Asians make up a small proportion of the population relative to Whites. Conclusively, findings confirm the hypothesis that Asian group size is negatively related to Asian-White biracial identification.

The percentage of Asians who are foreign-born is not related to Asian biracial identification with Whites at a statistically significant level. Geographic region, however, has a relatively strong impact on the dependent variable. Western Asians are over 45 percent more likely than Asians in other regions to report biracial identification with Whites.

Analysis Summary

Extending Peter Blau's conceptualization of intergroup relations to also include interracial identification demonstrates methodological support for using biracial identification as an indicator of social distance and also contributes to the collective understanding of the racial identification process. Indeed, 61.1 percent of the geographic variation in Asian biracial identification with Whites is attributable to exposure to Whites, equality with Whites in educational attainment, Asian group size relative to Whites, and geographic region. Asians are more likely to report biracial identification with Whites the more Asian social circles intersect with that of Whites because the more Asians and Whites have in common, the less race matters. But with the in-group being the default (per the theory), which in this case would be monoracial Asian identification, greater equality and larger Asian group size decreases the likelihood Asians report biracial identification because greater availability of same-status others in the minority group naturally breeds in-group allegiance. The R^2 for the multivariate model, coupled with statistically significant results for all major postulates in the hypothesized directions, provides significant overall support for extending Blau's macrostructural theory beyond intergroup relations to the context of intergroup identification.

DISCUSSION ON ASIAN-WHITE
BIRACIAL INCIDENCE FINDINGS

In this chapter, I borrowed from Peter Blau's macrostructural theory on intergroup relations and subsequent empirical scholarship on interracial marriage to assess the effects of macrostructural variables on the likelihood of Asian Americans reporting biracial identification with Whites on the 2010 U.S. Census. By evaluating the extent social forces known to influence interracial marriage also influence interracial identification, this study extends Blau's theory beyond explaining the likelihood two different-race people will marry to the likelihood one person will identify with two different races (but at the group-level, rather than the individual-level).

Blau's theory depends on the comparison of two groups in which one is a minority and the other is a majority. The theory lends itself to "race" as the demographic characteristic defining group membership, and empirical studies testing the theory consistently choose Whites as the majority group and either Blacks, Asians, or Hispanics as the minority group. As with most analyses of race in America, former tests of Blau's theory most commonly gravitate toward Blacks and Whites, and for good reason. Blacks have more social distance from Whites than any other racial group. They're the most segregated from Whites. They intermarry with Whites the least. They identify as half White far less than the odds would predict. The list goes on.

However, it is important to the interpretation of the Black model to also investigate Asian social distance from Whites because it sheds light on the magnitude of the situation. Comparison groups present an opportunity to capture relative standing in order to quantify distances in social hierarchy. Asians have experienced discrimination, segregation, and hate crimes at the hands of Whites. Many Asians were stripped of their assets and forced into concentration camps right here on American soil during World War II. They lost their businesses and their family farms. They were forced to drop out of school, and forfeit their homes. As a whole, however, wage gap data and real median household income data show that Asians have recovered from these historical wrong doings, at least economically (PayScale 2020; U.S. Census Bureau 2018).

This chapter examines the applicability of Blau's macrostructural theory of intergroup relations to Asians and Whites to determine if the theory's explanatory value can be extended beyond explaining interracial marriage, and also beyond the realm of Black and White. Indeed it does. As this chapter has demonstrated, the explanatory value of Blau's theory, which has been tested inside and out on interracial marriage, absolutely extends to interracial identification. This chapter also demonstrates that the theory's applicability remains steadfast beyond Black and White. Over 61 percent of the geographic variation in Asian biracial identification with Whites is attributable to Asian exposure to Whites, educational equality between Asians and Whites, Asian group size relative to Whites, and geographic region. This indicates evidence of some social distance between Asians and Whites.

Although 61 percent is considered quite strong in the social sciences, it cannot be overlooked that the exact same model applied to Blacks explains 30 percent more geographic variation in biracial identification with Whites. The difference in explanatory power between the two well-performing models confirms that Blacks are considerably more racially distant from Whites than Asians. This is not unexpected. Whereas over 13 percent of today's legal marriages are interracial (Lee and Bean 2007b), Asians far over-index on interracial marriage in America, with nearly one in three Asian Americans marrying out, mainly to Whites (Roth 2005). Blacks on the other hand are far less likely to interracially marry, especially with Whites. These trends, together with my findings, clearly confirm that Blacks are far more racially distanced from Whites than Asians.

Certain structural elements influence racial distance more than others. The extent social circles intersect with Whites is a much more impactful determinant of biracial identification for Blacks than for Asians. In other words, segregation for Blacks hinders biracial identification with Whites to a much greater degree than it does for Asians. The long-lasting effects of slavery seem to have solidified detrimental effects in a way that is definitive, making barriers to opportunity nearly impenetrable, and true interracial integration a nearly impossible dream.

But what we may also be seeing here is more simply that Asians are less segregated than Blacks. Segregation is more common among large minority groups (Park and Burgess 1921) and racial minority groups with recent active immigration flow (Castles and Miller 2003). And although Asians are growing much faster than Blacks due to immigration trends, and are indeed the fastest growing racial group in the United States, Asians are the least segregated racial group while Blacks are clearly the most (Farley 2011). This is true even in Los Angeles where the Asian group size is very large and racial discrimination against Asians is rife.

Group size also affects Black biracial identification with Whites more than it does for Asians. That is, larger Black group sizes deter Black identification with Whites much more than larger Asian group sizes deter Asian identification with Whites. While it is believed that the larger the group size, the more threatening the group to Whites (Blalock 1967), this effect seems to be quite a bit stronger when the group in question is Black.

Meanwhile, educational inequality influences Asian likelihood to identify as also White more than it does for Blacks. Inequality reflects socioeconomic disparities between the racial minority group and Whites. Educational inequality in particular reflects differences in status that are persistent. Consistent with Roth (2005), the more the local Asian group is educated at the same levels as Whites, the more Asians are likely to identify monoracially Asian.

In closing, this chapter further confirms the utility of Blau's theory of intergroup relations in explaining interracial identification in new ways after decades of qualitative research identifying highly personal and social psychological factors influencing one's racial identity, and much quantitative work assessing the influence of personal and familial demographics, social network compositions, and other meso-level factors on racial identity and identification. By adding macro-level factors to the list of known micro- and meso-level factors well-proven to influence interracial identification, this study fills a gap in our understanding of race in America.

I set out asking why some cities have greater biracial identification incidence than others. After answering that question in the previous chapter, and confirming that answer with this chapter, I then asked why different groups are affected by the same factors differently. For example, nearly as many Asians as Blacks identified as half White on the 2010 Census (1.6 million and 1.8 million, respectively) even though the total Asian American population is 2.4 smaller in number than the total Black population. Knowing that biracial identification is affected by the racial climate and its effects, the degree to which structural factors affect Asians differently than Blacks, and Blacks differently than Asians, has important policy implications. Yet too few racial identification studies analyze more than one racial pairing at a time. To overcome this gap in the literature, I applied the exact same research design used in the prior chapter (examining structural influence on the likelihood of biracial Blacks identifying as half White) to examine structural influence on the likelihood of biracial Asians identifying as half White in this chapter. This analytic design enabled direct comparisons, revealing quantifiable and statistically significant differences between the Black group and the Asian group in their relationship to the White group.

I'll repeat those last few words...*in their relationship to the White group.* Recent scholarship within the discipline of interraciality has criticized the larger body of interracial identity work for its Anglo-centricity (Washington 2017). Indeed, the overwhelming majority of biracial studies, and the theoretical frameworks from whence they came, have focused on those with partial White and partial Black heritage, by a landslide. A distant second most popular biracial group analyzed is Asian and White. This book seeks to overcome this gap in the literature by completing the trifecta with the following chapter. The relevance of macrostructural theory to non-White biracial groups, such as Black-Asians, will be tested to better understand interminority dynamics. The meaning of "minority" as a numerical construct will be contrasted with the idea of "minority" defined by oppression in the coming chapters.

NOTES

1. Note that Hispanic is considered an *ethnicity* by the U.S. Census Bureau, rather than a *racial category*.

2. As a dummy variable, region cannot be transformed because $\ln(0)$ is undefined.

Chapter 4

Structural Influence on Biracial Identification between Asians and Blacks

When the 2000 U.S. Census allowed respondents to describe themselves with more than one racial category for the first time, nearly 7 million did. By the 2010 Census, this figure had grown three times more than the total American population. Whereas the total number of people living in the United States grew 9.7 percent between 2000 and 2010, the number of people identifying with more than one race grew 32 percent.

Among 42 million Blacks (13.6 percent of the American population), more than 3 million Blacks identified as multiracial in 2010. Multiracial Blacks make up just over 7 percent of the total Black population. This is roughly half of what would be expected due to chance however, as the ratio of Blacks to non-Blacks is 0.16. In other words, odds would predict that nearly 16 percent of all Blacks would identify with another race, yet the figure is less than half that.

A very different dynamic is observed with Asians—in fact an equal and opposite dynamic. Among 17 million Asian Americans, 2.6 million identified as multiracial in 2010. Multiracial Asians make up over 15 percent of the total Asian American population. This is more than double what would be expected due to chance, as the ratio of Asians to non-Asians is 0.06. That is, odds would predict that about 6 percent of all Asian Americans would identify with another race, but more than 15 percent actually did. Asian Americans as a group are roughly a third the size of the Black population but are more than twice as likely to identify as multiracial.

I pointed out in previous chapters that Asians are more than twice as likely as Blacks to biracially identify with Whites and explain why. Here I point out that Asians are more than twice as likely as Blacks to biracially identify *with any race*. Davis (1991) estimates that as many as 70 percent of Blacks in America are multiracial. Yet only 7 percent of Blacks indicated that they are multiracial on the census. Responses to the census race question confirm that racial identification is indeed a choice (Harris and Sim 2002; Hirschman 2004; Masuoka 2011). Now the question becomes, which factors influence that choice? And why are different groups affected by the same factors differently?

The answer to the first question has been well-researched, in a sense. Decades of qualitative research has identified highly personal and social psychological factors influencing one's racial identity. This work has informed important racial identity frameworks used by other scholars deploying quantitative methods to confirm and build upon the body of knowledge in this discipline. Gathering large-scale data on biracial populations was a challenge before the 2000 Census. A recent surge of quantitative work takes advantage of this groundbreaking data source to assess the influence of personal and familial demographics, social network compositions, and other meso-level factors on racial identification at the individual, household, and sometimes even the group-level. Although many of these have peppered in macro-level factors such as segregation and group size, what has been missing is a macro-structural perspective asking why some cities have greater biracial identification incidence than others.

Chapter 2 aimed to fill this gap by answering that very question. Not only is racial identification influenced by micro- and meso-level factors, but chapter 2 finds that it is influenced by macro-level factors as well. We know from previous research that racial identity and identification is influenced by personal social psychological factors, personal sociodemographic factors, and immediate social setting/social network factors. Now we know that racial identification is also influenced by the broader urban composition where so many people of color live, as demonstrated in chapter 2.

To review, a city's segregation intensity influences biracial identification incidence in that city. How evenly higher educational attainment is distributed across racial groups in a city also influences biracial identification incidence in that city. The racial composition and nativity incidence of a city influences its biracial identification incidence. And the geographic region in which a city sits also influences the likelihood that the people living in it will identify biracially.

Racial identification is a choice. Chapter 2 adds new factors to the list of dynamics influencing that choice by addressing why Black biracial identification incidence with Whites is high in some cities and low in others. Much like empiricism on biracial marriage and other forms of interracial relations, biracial identification empiricism gravitates toward the Black-White divide. There are more published studies of Black-White multiracial identity and identification than any other multiracial pairing, by a landslide. Methodological convenience from large sample sizes aside, Blacks and

Whites are important groups to study together for many reasons. And with the killings of people like George Floyd, Breonna Taylor, and so many others at the hands of those sworn to serve and protect, this is true now more than ever.

But our broader understanding of racial identification and, importantly, what it says about social distance is limited if we can't answer the question of why different groups are affected by the same factors differently. Too few racial identification studies investigate more than one racial pairing. This book aims to fill that gap, beginning with chapter 3. I applied the exact same research design used in chapter 2 (examining structural influence on the likelihood of biracial Blacks to identify as half White) to examine the structural influence on the likelihood of biracial Asians to identify as half White in chapter 3. This analytic design enabled direct comparisons, revealing quantifiable and statistically significant differences between the Black group and the Asian group in their relationship to the White group. But why stop there?

The group of individuals who are both Black and Asian have previously been suggested as a fruitful area for future interracial identification studies (Campbell 2007; Lou, Lalonde and Wilson 2011; Williams and Thornton 1998; Wilton, Sanchez and Garcia 2013). Their "multiple marginalized status" makes this group particularly worth examining for policy implications (Washington 2017; Williams and Thornton 1998:258). For totally different reasons, a surge in attention toward this group has surfaced: "With nationwide protests against police brutality, rising incidents of anti-Asian racism, and the selection of Sen. Kamala Harris as the Democratic vice presidential nominee, race relations within and between the Asian American and Black communities have quickly shifted into focus" (Venkatraman and Lockhart 2020). One "Blasian" interviewed in the article specifically commented that the Black Lives Matter movement, coupled with the "pandemic-fueled discrimination" aimed at Asians, is an "exhausting" interracial nexus to embody. Analyzing differences in the effects of macrostructural contexts on the intersection of these groups is totally uncharted territory and is the focus of this chapter. This design allows me to contrast the meaning of minority, defined numerically, with the meaning of minority, defined by sustained oppression.

Whereas in chapter 2 I took the count of biracial individuals who indicated both Black and White on the census and divided by the count of the entire Black population, in chapter 3 I measure the prevalence of Asians who are half White by counting biracial individuals who indicated both Asian and White and then dividing by the count of the entire Asian population. Here, I measure both the prevalence of Blacks who are half Asian, and the prevalence of Asians who are half Black. Compared to 13.0 percent of Americans that are Black in any racial combination, 0.4 percent of Blacks claim Black-Asian biracial identification.[1] In contrast, the percentage of the Asian population claiming biracial Black is only 1.1 percent, as compared to 5.6 percent of Americans that are Asian in any racial combination.

To evaluate whether social forces known to influence interracial marriage also influence biracial identification among those who are both Asian and Black, macrostructural parameters across 363 metropolitan areas will be examined. Macrostructural factors vary geographically, and not coincidently, so do Black and Asian biracial identification incidences. Indeed, there is considerable geographic variation in the prevalence of Blacks that identify as half Asian, and the prevalence of Asians that identify as half Black, in the United States. Metropolitan areas range from 0.1 percent of Blacks reporting half Asian identification in Pine Bluff, Arkansas (where Blacks represent 48.4 percent of the population), to 3.1 percent in Salinas, California (where Blacks represent 4.0 percent of the population). Meanwhile, metropolitan areas range from 0.1 percent of Asians reporting half Black identification in Sheboygan, Wisconsin (where Asians are nearly proportionately represented, 5.0 percent), to 7.1 percent in Hinesville-Fort Steward, Georgia (where Asians represent 2.8 percent of the population).

This and other distinctions across metropolitan areas suggest that underlying structural differences could be affecting the likelihood of biracial identification. Borrowing from prior theoretical and empirical scholarship on mixed-race marriage, this study explores how urban structural factors affecting intergroup relations impact the likelihood racial minorities report biracial identification with each other. Specifically, I repurpose Peter Blau's macrostructural theory of intergroup relations, and the interracial marriage empirical scholarship emerging from this framework, to assess the effects of macrostructural variables on the likelihood of Black and Asian Americans reporting biracial identification with each other in this chapter.

STRUCTURAL FACTORS AFFECTING
ASIAN AND BLACK RELATIONSHIPS

Intergroup relations are often investigated through the lens of exchange, assimilation, or opportunity-structure perspectives. The opportunity-structure perspective rests on Simmel's (1908) notion of over-lapping social circles in which each social circle is based on a demographic (or lifestyle) characteristic. The characteristic that is most salient is the social circle in which the person feels the most belonging. This becomes their core group. People generally prefer to interact with members of their own core demographic group. However, Simmel argues that meaningful social relationships can happen between people from different groups if they are similar in many other ways.

If other social circles significantly intersect, shared commonalities become the grounds on which social relationships can be formed despite belonging to different core groups.

Peter Blau adds to Simmel's perspective in his macrostructural theory of intergroup relations (Blau 1977, 1994) by arguing that various structural factors help and hinder opportunities to fulfill in-group preferences, making intergroup relations more likely under certain conditions. The first pertains to the degree to which commonalities are shared. Keep in mind, this is a macrostructural view, so this is the degree to which there is common ground *between groups* in a given geographic area. Blau theorizes that spatial opportunities for contact help or hinder the likelihood of intergroup relations. Second is the numerical availability of in-group associates that have similar status. When there are less in-group individuals of similar status, there are proportionately more out-group individuals of otherwise similar status. The third is the group's relative size. When minority groups grow to be quite large, they tend to become segregated, both geographically and socially. They also become homogeneous and delineated, limiting contact and the extent any characteristics are shared with the out-group.

Blau's macrostructural theory of intergroup relations can utilize most any demographic variable to delineate groups, but the theory clearly lends itself to race as a salient characteristic defining in-group and out-group. The theory has been used to explain the probability of several different types of interracial relations, including interracial contact, conflict, and marriage. These studies have tested the theory's various postulates, including those centered on demographic consolidation (i.e., the degree to which there is common ground *between groups* in a given geographic area), inequality (i.e., the degree to which in-group associates of similar status are available), and group size (relative to the majority group size).

Demographic Consolidation among Asians and Blacks

The theory contends that relations can happen between members of different races if most of their other social circles intersect. That is, when race is less correlated with other demographics, interracial contact is more likely. Race, however, tends to have strong correlations with many other characteristics, thereby inhibiting chances that members of two racial groups share the social circles on which these characteristics are formed. When racial salience in heightened, intolerance of dissimilar others is also heightened. These sociocultural conditions breed antagonistic allegiance in opposition to institutional and interpersonal racism. Together these dynamics consolidate sociodemographic characteristics and homogenize the minority group, making interracial relations less likely as social circles for members of different racial groups fail to intersect in a healthy way.

Segregation can be described as geographical confinement creating cultural and social barriers that ultimately serve to constrain group characteristics that would otherwise vary. Segregation limits the number of similarities between racial groups, and is known to be especially compounded in cities where the minority group is numerically large enough to be perceived as a threat by the majority group (Blalock 1967; Massey and Denton 1993; Waters 1999; Wilson 1980). Given these factors, it cleanly operationalizes Blau's theoretical postulate around demographic consolidation and its directionally negative relationship to intergroup relations.

Inequality between Asians and Blacks

The theory assumes people prefer to interact with members of their own racial group so long as they share some other status. The idea is that people prefer to marry within their own race, *and also* prefer to marry within their own social class, or at the very least, someone with a similar level of education. Conceivably, couples with similar educational backgrounds will have much more in common and are probably more likely to get along as a result of sharing certain thought systems than couples where one partner is quite educated and the other is rather undereducated. Now, imagine a hypothetical racial minority group in a hypothetical city. Within this racial group, there are just a few highly educated individuals. Blau postulates that these highly educated minorities will be more likely to marry outside their racial group in the interest of pairing up with someone that they have more in common with intellectually. This hypothetical scenario describes a city characterized by educational inequality between racial groups.

In a different hypothetical city with educational equality between races, racial minorities will be well-represented in the same educational tiers as the majority group. In this scenario, there is a sufficient pool of members from the racial minority group represented in even the most elite educational tiers. The theory assumes that these highly educated racial minorities will prefer to marry other highly educated members of their own racial group. In this way, the theory postulates, educational equality between races increases the likelihood of same-race marriage (a phenomenon which is unique to the macro-perspective). But if the racial minority group is really small, no degree of educational equality between racial groups will create a sufficient pool of same-race members in the elite educational tiers, and those highly educated minorities will be more likely to marry-out than to marry-in. For this reason, relative group size must be included in the model.

Group Size of Asians, Relative to Blacks and
Group Size of Blacks, Relative to Asians

The theory concludes that interracial relations are more likely among members of groups that are numerically small relative to the majority group because numerically limited in-group options make out-group options statistically more probable. The effect is particularly apparent in race applications because smaller racial groups tend to be more heterogeneous and therefore are more distributed across various social dimensions. This theoretical construct is fairly straight forward and is therefore operationalized with a simple calculation of racial minority group size, relative to the comparison group size.

Structural factors such as demographic consolidation, inequality, and group size have been theorized to affect the likelihood of relations with different-race others and have repeatedly been shown to affect the likelihood of interracial marriage. Macrostructural scholars have saturated the topic of Black-White intermarriage and Asian-White intermarriage. With only 15 percent of new marriages in America being interracial as of the 2010 Census, and most of those between Blacks and Whites, and Asians and Whites, there's a big gaping hole in our understanding of racial distance—and that is the distance between two racial minority groups. With double-minority intermarriage much less common than minority-White intermarriage, and with marriage considerably less likely among interracial couples in the first place, insufficient sample size across geographies is one reason that non-White, interracial marriage studies have not emerged in the literature through the opportunity-structure perspective. Perhaps another reason is that race scholars are guilty of Anglo-centricity. So much race scholarship focuses on groups and behaviors that are seen as a departure from White conformity, and by focusing so much of our attention here, we are in fact reinforcing White as the standard. Meanwhile, non-White interracial phenomena are being ignored (Washington 2017).

An understanding of social distance between minority racial groups is as critical as ever in 2020. This is a time when the pandemic in the United States is being blamed on Asian Americans, who are consequently getting spit on and beaten by strangers on the street. This is also a time when Blacks are making it clear that they've had enough. Many people are starting to listen. Many are not. 2020 was a year of racial eruption. Will the society that emerges from the ashes be a nation divided by White/non-White? Or does the staying power of hypodescent norms insure a Black/non-Black divide in the American racial hierarchy? There are actually several other possibilities as well, but asking questions this book doesn't answer is outside of the scope of this discussion. Rather, the point is that if minority-minority interracial marriage sample size can't manage robust analysis, our society still needs to understand inter-minority social distance dynamics and scholars should move onto adjacent contexts with data sources that *can*.

Contemporary American society is characterized by widespread cohabitation, partnerships not legally recognized as marriage, divorce, and non-marital childbearing. Compared to same-race couples, interracial couples are less likely to marry in the first place and less likely stay married if they do. Combined with the fact that marriage data is insufficient in helping us understand inter-minority dynamics from a macrostructural perspective, we must find another empirical path forward in order to advance the discipline.

In the same way that interracial marriage incidence has reflected racial integration in the past, biracial identification incidence may represent a more stable indicator of integration in today's society. Biracial identification can also shed light on what today may be described as the dark side of the moon: quantifiable dynamics influencing inter-minority race relations. The flexibility of the new census race question more accurately tallies variations in racial groups than ever before. This gives demographers like me the opportunity to leverage data on biracial *people*, rather than data on biracial *marriage*, to proxy social distance. It also gives me the opportunity to look at double-minority racial identification at scale. This study applies concepts drawn from Blau's macrostructural theory of intergroup relations, and the copious empiricism testing the theory on interracial marriage between Whites and racial minorities, to understand how structure influences biracial identification between two racial minority groups in the United States: Blacks and Asians.

FACTORS AFFECTING ASIAN AND BLACK
INTERRACIAL IDENTIFICATION

If the availability of data has presented a challenge to the understanding of interracial marriage in America, it has presented a far greater challenge to the understanding of interracial identification. Before recent times, most of the work in interracial identity was qualitative and conducted with desperately small sample sizes. This is what was available at the time. Frameworks for understanding racial identity development emerged and were tested and retested by scholars who painstakingly chipped away at an iceberg of a topic. This work paved the way for strides in scholarly contributions from larger-scale, quantitative data on interracial individuals, households, and groups. Qualitative work continues to add tremendous value to the discipline by helping to explain "the why" behind "the what" that is observed through more quantitative methods. Importantly, qualitative methods are and will continue to be the mainstay of inter-minority scholarship, as there is so much foundational work to be done here. Meanwhile, published quantitative studies on biracial individuals and groups that are both Asian and Black are few in number today.² None examine racial identification through a fully macrostructural lens.

Highlights from the studies especially relevant to this paper are parsed together with findings from studies observing Black-White and Asian-White biracial individuals to reveal two key insights. First is with regard to how hypodescent norms will perform in a double-minority model. Whereas Blacks are subjected to hypodescents, Asians are not necessarily (Brunsma 2005; Masuoka 2011; Tafoya et al. 2005; Townsend et al. 2012; Xie and Goyette 1997). When forced to choose one race, biracial Black-Whites usually default to Black, while biracial Asian-Whites usually default to White (Tafoya et al. 2005). This begs the question of whether hypodescents will or will not influence the racial identification of individuals who are both Black and Asian. As it turns out, Black-Asians do experience pressure from hypodescents (Williams and Thornton 1998). When forced to choose one racial category, Black-Asians are more likely to choose monoracial Black than monoracial Asian (Parker et al. 2004; Xie and Goyette 1997). "Blasians should be afforded the same access to symbolic identities as Whiteness affords, but they are not, because as people of color they are constrained by narrowly defined extant categories of racialization" (Washington 2017: 10). This initially suggests that cultural oppression trumps numerical underrepresentation in its impact on the racial minority experience.

Second is with regard to how double-minority respondents indicate their racial identification when given the option to "check all that apply." Whereas Black-Whites are overwhelmingly more likely to identify monoracially Black even when given the choice to check more than one box, Asian-Whites are equally likely to identify biracially as they are to identify monoracially Asian or monoracially White (Roth 2005; Xie and Goyette 1997). This begs the question of whether individuals who are both Black and Asian will or will not default to a monoracial designation. As it turns out, Black-Asians do not default to monoracial identification. When given the choice to identify with one race or more than one race, Black-Asians are more likely to check more than one race (Williams and Thornton 1998), providing support for the *protean identity* model. In fact, Black-Asians are just as likely as White-Asians to identify as biracial (Williams 1992). This is in unambiguous contrast to the difference in biracial identification likelihood between Black-Whites and Asian-Whites, suggesting that perhaps Blasians do have some access to the symbolic identities afforded by Whiteness after all.

This brings us back to the concept of hypodescents. More commonly referred to as "the one-drop rule," *hypodescents* is defined as a societal phenomenon that commands biracial individuals default to the identity or identification of their minority half (see Davis 1991). In the case of individuals who are both Black and Asian, which is their minority half? This simple inquiry questions whether the definition of "minority" is based on oppression or group size. Although this is such a significant question, there are so few studies to answer it. The first key insight above finds that when individuals are not given the option to "check all that apply," yes, hypodescents triumphs over the Black-Asian racial identification process. But when individuals are given the option to "check all that apply," no, hypodescents *does not* triumph over the Black-Asian racial identification process. Over the years I have seen conjectures arguing that hypodescents only applies to Blacks (and not other racial minorities). But taken together, I'd argue that hypodescents only applies to non-Whites.

In the 2010 Census, the stark difference between the percentage of Asians that identified as half Black (from this point forward called *Asian-Blacks*) and the percentage of Blacks that identified as half Asian (from this point forward called *Black-Asians*) is astounding. Asians are just over a third the size of Blacks but nearly thrice as likely to identify with Blacks than Blacks are to identify with Asians. Among 42.0 million Blacks (13.6 percent of the American population) in 2010, only 0.2 million, or 0.4 percent of the total Black population, were identified as half Asian, compared with 1.1 percent (of the 17.3 million Asians in America) who identified as half Black. The question is why, and a further examination of the minority-minority biracial group in this chapter will help unpack inter-minority dynamics often challenged by insufficient sample sizes or overlooked by a general predisposition toward White biracial groups.

HYPOTHESIZING THE INFLUENCE OF STRUCTURE ON ASIAN AND BLACK BIRACIAL IDENTIFICATION

Peter Blau's macrostructural theory postulates that although minorities prefer relations with members of their own group, certain structural conditions increase the likelihood that they'll seek relations outside the group. Considerable quantitative empiricism tested the theory with much success using interracial marriage as the outcome variable. These macrostructural scholars saturated the topic of Black-White intermarriage, and also sufficiently covered the topic of Asian-White intermarriage. Among the few that examine group differences in intermarriage incidence, most focus on group differences in intermarriage with Whites. This leaves a real gap examining inter-minority dynamics.

Meanwhile, a completely separate stream of scholarly work developed and tested theories on the topic of interracial identity and identification. Considerable qualitative discourse on this topic lines the shelves of my home office library. Cumulative findings emerged over many decades from a multitude of rich, smaller sample size studies. These have provided much needed context enabling future empirical work. But even after the new "check all that apply" race question made its debut on the 2000 Census, offering sufficient sample size for examining groups beyond those identifying as part White, biracial identification among non-Whites has not been the subject of many a quantitative study.

In this book, I borrow from a macrostructural theory of intergroup relations and its accompanying empirical scholarship on the structural determinants of interracial marriage. I test whether the theory can be extended beyond interracial marriage to interracial people. I evaluate whether groups of interracial people might be a better social distance indicator than interracial marriage today. I also simultaneously test several different interracial groups in order to estimate differences in social distance between races. I then reference a totally different body of scholarship dissecting the interracial identity experience to explain some of those differences. The real contribution of this chapter in particular is that few macrostructural marriage demographers and racial identification scholars have pursued an understanding of double-minority groups. Surely the relationship between racial minority groups is significant for many of the same reasons as the relationship between Whites and racial minority groups. This intersection may also reveal that the relationship between groups is significant for unique reasons that a focus on Whiteness misses. American society is arguably characterized by a racial hierarchy that is far more complex than the preponderance of studies focused on White/non-White or Black/non-Black dichotomies would suggest.

In this section, I repurpose macrostructural theory, and the interracial marriage empirical scholarship emerging from this framework, to assess the effects of macrostructural variables on the likelihood of Black and Asian Americans reporting biracial identification with each other. After success in the previous two chapters testing whether factors facilitating interracial marriage also encourage interracial identification, I again hypothesize that:

H_1. The more social circles between Asians and Blacks intersect, the greater the likelihood Asians will report biracial identification with Blacks and Blacks will report biracial identification with Asians.

H_2. The greater the educational equality between Asians and Blacks, the greater the likelihood Asians will report monoracial Asian identification and Blacks will report monoracial Black identification.

H_3. The smaller the Asian group size relative to Blacks, the greater the likelihood Asians will report biracial identification with Blacks. Similarly, the smaller the Black group size relative to Asians, the greater the likelihood Blacks will report biracial identification with Asians.

H$_4$. The model positioning Blacks as the racial minority will be stronger than
   the model positioning Asians as the racial minority.

DATA AND METHODS

Metropolitan areas have been the primary pallet for interracial contact since
the antebellum period (Wilson 1980). Therefore, metropolitan areas including
MSAs and metropolitan NECTAs are the natural units of analysis for measuring interracial contact, and conceivably, interracial identification. There are 363
metropolitan areas in the continental United States. All are used in this analysis.

OLS regression is used to analyze these data. Blau's theory depends on the
comparison of two groups in which one is a minority and the other is a majority. Because the analysis in this chapter investigates two minority groups, two
separate models are devised in order to be able to position each group as the
minority. The first model, which I refer to as the *Asian-Black* model, situates
Asians as the minority. The second model, which I refer to as the *Black-Asian*
model, situates Blacks as the minority. My conclusions then compare models
to contrast the meaning of "minority" as Blau intended (numerically) with the
idea of "minority" defined by oppression.

Dependent Variables: Asian-Black and Black-
Asian Biracial Identification Incidences

For each city, the percentage of all Asian Americans identifying as half Asian
is calculated using data reported in Census Summary File 1. The percentage of
all Blacks who claim Asian as part of a biracial identification is also calculated
for comparison. Whereas 1.1 percent of Asians indicated biracial Black, only
0.4 percent of Blacks indicated biracial Asian. Percentages of Asians claiming
Asian-Black identification range from 0.1 percent in Sheboygan, Wisconsin
(where Asians are almost proportionately represented, 5.0 percent), to 7.1
percent in Hinesville-Fort Steward, Georgia (where Asians represent but 2.8
percent of the population). Percentages of Blacks claiming biracial Asian range
from 0.1 percent claiming Black-Asian identification in Pine Bluff, Arkansas
(where Blacks represent half the population, 48.4 percent), to 3.1 percent in
Salinas, California (where Blacks represent 4.0 percent of the metro population).

Independent Variables: Structural Factors
Affecting Asians and Blacks

Several structural variables are hypothesized to explain the variance in biracial identification prevalence across geographies. These include interracial
exposure, racial equality, and relative group size.

Asian Exposure to Blacks and Black Exposure to Asians

Exposure of one racial group to another is measured by the exposure index. This index measures the probability of interaction between Asians and Blacks by taking the average percentage of an area that is Black, within the neighborhood (i.e., census tract) of an Asian American, and again by taking the average percentage of an area that is Asian, within the neighborhood of a Black American. Both the average percentage of an area that is Asian within the census tract of a Black person and the average percentage of an area that is Black within the census tract of an Asian person are calculated to understand the extent to which Asian exposure to Blacks, and Black exposure to Asians, affects biracial identification between Asians and Blacks. The exposure index for each metropolitan area can theoretically range from 0 (indicating no exposure between Asians and Blacks), to a number equal to the proportion of the population that is Black in a city with only one Asian American, or the proportion of the population that is Asian in a city with only one Black person. Both exposure scores were calculated from 2010 Census data for each metropolitan area and are available from the University of Michigan Population Studies Center. Scores for Asian exposure to Blacks range from 0.2 in Wenatchee, Washington, to 40.6 in Hinesville-Fort Steward, Georgia. Scores for Black exposure to Asians range from 0.3 in Muskegon-Norton Shores, Michigan, to 30.2 in San Jose-Sunnyvale-Santa Clara, California.

Racial Equality between Asians and Blacks

For each metropolitan area in the 2007–2011 ACS, chi-square is calculated for the relationship between race and education by dividing the raw chi-square term by the maximum chi-square value (and then multiplying by 100). Because chi-square indicates the extent census frequencies deviate from what would be expected if race and education were independent, higher scores indicate greater deviation from independence between race and education, implying educational attainment is more dependent upon race. The calculated expression is subtracted from 100 to reverse the scale such that higher scores indicate greater educational parity (i.e., education is less dependent on race) between Asians and Blacks. Scores range from 0.06 in Anderson, Indiana, where Asians and Blacks are divided by education, to 43.37 in Morgantown, West Virginia, where Asians and Blacks are more proportionately represented in each educational attainment category.

Asian Group Size, Relative to Blacks and
Black Group Size, Relative to Asians

Relative group size is measured by the number of Asians per thousand single-race Blacks, and again by the number of Blacks per thousand single-race

Asians, depending on which group is positioned as the minority in the model. Data for these calculations are available for each metropolitan area in Census Summary File 1. The ratio of Asians to Blacks ranges from Pine Bluff, Arkansas at the low end, to San Jose-Sunnyvale-Santa Clara, California at the high end. The ratio of Blacks to Asians ranges from San Jose-Sunnyvale-Santa Clara, California at the low end, to Rocky Mount, North Carolina at the high end.

Control Variables

The percentage of the Asian population foreign-born, the percentage of the Black population foreign-born, and geographic region help isolate the effects of the main structural features under analysis. Five-year estimates of the number of foreign-born Asians and foreign-born Blacks are available from the 2007–2011 ACS Table B16005, A-I. These measures are calculated as the percentage of total single-race Asians that are foreign-born, with ranges from 46.3 percent in Idaho Falls, Idaho, to 91.3 percent in Anderson, Indiana, and again as the percentage of total single-race Blacks that are foreign-born, which ranges from 0.0 percent where there are no reported foreign-born Blacks in Sandusky, Ohio, Kokomo, Indiana or Coeur d'Alene, Idaho, to 60.4 percent in Fargo, North Dakota-Minnesota.

Just as regional variations shaped interracial identification with Whites in previous chapters, regional variations are also expected to shape interracial identification in this chapter. In chapter 2, examining biracial Black-Whites, I designated the South as the reference region. In chapter 3, examining biracial Asian-Whites, I designated the West as the reference region. This chapter examines the incidence of biracial people who are part Black and part Asian, so the question becomes which region to use as the reference group in the dummy variable. There are some nuances to consider. From a historical standpoint, anti-miscegenation laws didn't apply to minority-minority inter-racial marriages in some states, and California in the West is a prize example (Kitano et al. 1984). Meanwhile, most Asian-Black intermarriages today are in the South (Heaton and Jacobson 2000). Whereas the longest and most con-centrated history of Black discrimination is in the South (Wilson 1980), the longest and most concentrated history of Asian discrimination is in the West (JACL 2008; Kitano et al. 1984). Therefore, I use a different dummy vari-able depending on which minority group is positioned as the minority in the model. When Asians are positioned as the minority group, regions are coded into dummy variables where the South, Midwest, and Northeast are coded as 1, and the West is coded as 0 to indicate the reference group. When Blacks are the minority group in the model, the West, Midwest, and Northwest are coded as 1, and the South is coded as 0 to indicate the reference group.

Analytic Design

All variables are logged. This corrects for non-linearity and skewness to the right, and helps standardize the effect of different-sized metropolitan areas in the sample and differently scaled test variables in the model. Logging also circumvents the need for interaction terms. Once natural log transformations are performed on all variables except region,[3] these data meet regression assumptions and OLS regression was performed.

STRUCTURAL INFLUENCE ON DOUBLE-MINORITY BIRACIAL IDENTIFICATION

The average percentage (untransformed) of Asians reporting Asian-Black biracial identification across 363 metropolitan areas is 1.5 percent, with 0.012 standard deviations.[4] In comparison, the average percentage of Blacks reporting Black-Asian identification across metropolitan areas is 0.6 percent, with .006 standard deviations.[5] The greatest regional representation of Asians reporting biracial identification with Blacks is in the South (2.2 percent), where the smallest percentage of Blacks report biracial identification with Asians (0.3 percent). Similarly, the greatest regional representation of Blacks reporting biracial identification with Asians is in the West (1.4 percent), where the smallest percentage of Asians report biracial identification with Blacks (0.9 percent). Meanwhile, a similar proportion of Asians report being half Black in the Midwest (1.2 percent) as in the Northeast (1.1 percent). Similarly, 0.4 percent of Blacks identified as half Asian in both the Midwest and the Northeast. For comparison, Asians are most likely to report half White identification in the West (see chapter 3), whereas Asians are least likely to report half Black identification in the West (this chapter). The regional ranking in percentage of Blacks claiming Black-Asian identification mimics that of Blacks claiming Black-White identification (see chapter 2).

The correlation matrix and descriptive statistics associated with biracial identification in 363 metropolitan areas in the continental United States are shown in table 2.2 for both Asian-Blacks and Black-Asians. The percentage of Asians reporting Asian-Black biracial identification correlates fairly strongly with all explanatory variables. Similarly, the percentage of Blacks reporting Black-Asian biracial identification correlates fairly strongly with all explanatory variables, with the exception of equality. These findings preliminarily support the central research question: macrostructural variables influencing biracial marriage also influence biracial identification, even among non-White, double-minority groups. This is true regardless of which minority group is positioned as the minority in the model.

Bivariate Regression Analysis

The bivariate relationship between biracial identification and each explanatory variable of the model is displayed in table 2.3 for both Asian-Blacks and
Black-Asians. Whereas Asian exposure to Blacks explains 49.5 percent of
the geographic variation in the percentage of Asians claiming Asian-Black
biracial identification, Black exposure to Asians explains 41.6 percent of
the geographic variation in the percentage of Blacks claiming Black-Asian
biracial identification. Consistent with interracial relations theory, exposure
between Asians and Blacks is related to biracial identification in a positive
direction; greater Asian exposure to Blacks increases the percentage of Asian
biracial identification with Blacks, and greater Black exposure to Asians
likewise increases the percentage of Black biracial identification with Asians.
I would consider these explanatory powers (49.5 percent and 41.6 percent)
to be fairly within range of one another. Although the roughly 8 percent difference here is significant, the difference doesn't necessarily warrant further
attention because the bivariate view is a preparatory step in advance of the
multivariate view.

Meanwhile, racial equality explains 19.3 percent of the geographic
variation in the Asian-Black model but is not statistically significant in the
Black-Asian model. Greater educational equality between Asians and Blacks
decreases biracial identification among Asians but not necessarily among
Blacks. Again, at the bivariate level, this finding doesn't necessarily fail to
support the theory, which requires a multivariate approach given the influence of group size on both exposure and especially equality. Nonetheless, I
briefly present the bivariate results here for the purpose of other researchers
interested in replicating and hopefully improving upon this research design.

Lastly, group size is negatively related to biracial identification in both
models, just as the theory would have suggested had the theorist considered
the application of biracial identification. When the group size of one race is
small relative to the other, biracial identification incidence is greater than
when the minority group size is large. Asian group size relative to Blacks
explains 53.2 percent of the variation across cities in Asians reporting half
Black identification, while Black group size relative to Asians explains 65.9
percent of the variation in Blacks reporting half Asian identification.

Control variables are also statistically significant in both models. However
there are some interesting findings when compared to each model's half-
White counterpart (presented in chapter 2 for Blacks and chapter 3 for
Asians). Whereas the percentage of Asian Americans that are foreign-born
is negatively related to Asian-White biracial identification incidence, the
percentage of Asian Americans that are foreign-born is positively related
to Asian-Black biracial identification incidence. This means that cities with

greater percentages of Asian Americans who are foreign-born have lower percentages of Asians identifying as half White, and greater percentages of Asians identifying as half Black. Meanwhile, the Black-Asian model performs similarly as the Black-White model when it comes to the influence of nativity on interracial identification at the macro-level; the percentage of Black Americans that are foreign-born is positively related to Black biracial identification with Asians, just as it is to Black biracial identification with Whites. That is, cities with greater percentages of Black Americans foreign-born have greater percentages of Blacks identifying as half Asian, and greater percentages of Blacks identifying as half White. Finally, Asians in the West are less likely to claim Asian-Black biracial identification than in other regions, just as Blacks in the South are less likely to claim Black-Asian biracial identification than in other regions.

Multiple Regression Analysis

The simultaneous regression of biracial identification incidence on all explanatory variables in the models is displayed in table 2.3 for both Asian-Blacks and Black-Asians. Whereas all variables in the Asian-Black multivariate model significantly contribute to biracial identification incidence (with the exception of the nativity control variable), all variables in the Black-Asian multivariate model significantly contribute to biracial identification incidence (with the exception of the region control variable). The full Asian-Black model accounts for 66.8 percent of the variation across cities in Asian biracial identification with Blacks across cities, and the full Black-Asian model accounts for 72.7 percent of the variation in Black biracial identification with Asians across cities.

The first hypothesis predicts that greater Asian exposure to Blacks elicits greater Asian-Black identification incidence, and greater Black exposure to Asians elicits greater Black-Asian identification incidence. Exposure strongly performs as expected in both models, even with the effects of educational equality, group size, and control variables parsed away. A partial Black heritage among Asian Americans flourishes when Asians have more exposure to Blacks. And a partial Asian heritage among Black Americans flourishes when Blacks have more exposure to Asians. This suggests that greater exposure may inspire greater identification with both groups, perhaps signifying less social distance between races. Conversely, when exposure between Asians and Blacks is limited, monoracial identification is more prevalent, conceivably due to geographic, social, and cultural boundaries characteristic of segregated communities.

The second hypothesis predicts metropolitan areas with greater equality in education between Asians and Blacks have lower likelihoods of Asians identifying as half Black and Blacks identifying as half Asian. As expected, equality is negatively related to biracial identification incidence. If Asians and Blacks are represented in each educational attainment tier proportionately, same-race unions would be more likely because each racial minority group would have greater exposure to others that have similar qualities that accompany social class in their own racial group. Along the same line of reasoning, it is not surprising that educational equality also decreases biracial identification incidence between Asians and Blacks. That is, as each racial minority group becomes more proportionately represented along the distribution of educational categories, biracial identification incidence between Asians and Blacks decreases.

The third hypothesis predicts that members of smaller Asian groups relative to Blacks are more likely to identify as half Black, and members of smaller Black groups relatives to Asians are more likely to identify as half Asian. Consistent with biracial marriage studies where members of smaller racial minority groups are more likely to marry majority group members due to limited same-race options, biracial identification with Blacks is more prevalent when Asians make up a smaller proportion of the population. Likewise, biracial identification with Asians is more prevalent when Blacks make up a smaller proportion of the population. Conclusively, the hypothesis that Asian group size is negatively related to Asian-Black biracial identification incidence, and Black group size is negatively related to Black-Asian biracial identification, is confirmed.

As mentioned, the percentage of Asians who are foreign-born is not related to Asian biracial identification with Blacks at a statistically significant level, mirroring the Asian-White model described in chapter 3. However, the percentage of Blacks who are foreign-born is positively related to Black biracial identification with Asians, mirroring the Black-White model described in chapter 2. In the case of Blacks, cultural appreciation for diverse populations seems to facilitate biracial identification, but the same is not true of Asians. Geographic region has a relatively strong impact on the dependent variable in the Asian-Black model, but has no statistically significant value in the Black-Asian model. That is, the South affects the likelihood Blacks will identify as half White, but not the likelihood Blacks will identify as half Asian.

Analysis Summary

Extending Peter Blau's macrostructural conceptualization of intergroup relations to also include interracial identification demonstrates methodological support for using biracial identification incidence as an indicator of social distance. Indeed, 66.8 percent of the variation across cities in Asian biracial identification with Blacks is attributable to exposure to Blacks, equality with

Blacks in educational attainment, Asian group size relative to Blacks, and geographic region. Similarly, 72.7 percent of the variation across cities in Black biracial identification with Asians is attributable to exposure to Asians, equality with Asians in educational attainment, Black group size relative to Asians, and Black nativity.

Beyond extending Blau's theory to a new application evaluating social distance between two groups, these analyses also contribute to the collective understanding of the racial identification process by testing more than one racial pairing. This enables important comparisons between groups. Importantly, this analytic design steps into the great unknown by quantitatively examining geographic variation in non-White, double-minority biracial identification incidence in the United States. The theory postulates that people prefer relations with their own group. In the context of marriage, that means that same-race marriage is the default. And by extension, monoracial identification would be the default in the context of this new racial identification application. Just as greater equality and larger group sizes have been shown to decrease the likelihood of interracial marriage in past studies, this work finds that greater equality and larger group sizes also decrease the likelihood Asians and Blacks report interracial identification with one another. The more Asian and Black social circles intersect with one another, the more likely Asians are to report biracial identification with Blacks, and the more likely Blacks are to report biracial identification with Asians. The R^2 for both multivariate models, coupled with statistically significant results for all major postulates in the hypothesized direction, provides significant validation extending Blau's macrostructural theory.

DISCUSSION ON ASIAN-BLACK AND BLACK-ASIAN BIRACIAL INCIDENCE FINDINGS

Interracial marriage is an indication of declining social distance between races (Fu and Heaton 2000; Kalmijn 1998; Kalmijn and Van Tubergen 2010; Lee and Bean 2004; Lichter and Qian 2005; Qian et al. 2012; Suro 1999; Zhang and Vanhook 2009). Like interracial marriage, interracial identification has also been called an indicator of declining social distance between races (Bean and Stevens 2003; Bratter 2007; Lee and Bean 2004), eroding the racial hierarchy (Gans 2007; Wright et al. 2003) or at least circumventing it (Roth 2005). This book examines whether similar things that influence interracial marriage for each racial group also influence interracial identification for that group. The challenge is that most interracial marriage studies only look at one racial pairing, limiting our ability to directly identify group differences. Those that do include more than one racial pairing most often select partial White pairings only. These studies contrast Black interracial trends with Asian interracial trends as if the two never overlap.

Nevertheless, a brief review of how different dynamics affect each group's intermarriage likelihood can help shed some light on findings once the two minority groups are paired together as they are in this chapter. Let's start with residential segregation. Marriage demographers have found that segregation strongly works against Black intermarriage. In this book, I re-examine this phenomenon by measuring the influence of interracial exposure (as the inverse of residential segregation) on interracial identification incidence. Consistent with interracial marriage studies where Blacks exposed or other racial groups (which are almost unanimously White) are found to be more likely to interracially marry, I find that when Black groups are more exposed to other racial groups they are also more likely to identify interracially with those groups. Black-Asians are no exception; the more Blacks are exposed to Asians, the more likely Blacks are to identify as half Asian. This means that racial segregation between Blacks and Asians works against interracial identification incidence just as racial segregation has been found to work against Black interracial marriage in the marriage demography literature.

Meanwhile, the impact of residential segregation on Asian intermarriage has been mixed (see Hwang et al. 1994; Qian et al. 2012). In this chapter, however, I find clear evidence that the more Asians are exposed to Blacks, the more likely they are to identify as half Black. The multivariate coefficient for measuring the influence of residential segregation in the Asian-Black model is considerably greater than that in the Black-Asian model; Black exposure to Asians is less likely to encourage Blacks to identify as half Asian than Asian exposure to Blacks is to encourage Asians to identify as half Black. This suggests that residential segregation impacts Black integration much more than it impacts Asian integration.

Let's now move on to educational equality. The theory holds that in mostly less educated racial groups, the relatively few members that are more highly educated will be more challenged to find an equally educated mate within their own racial group. In more highly educated racial groups, the opposite is true; the many educated members of the racial group will have a good-sized selection pool of similarly educated, same-race mate options to choose from, and according to the theory, will be more likely to form relationships with these same-race peers than they will be to form interracial relationships.

Like residential segregation, marriage demographers have found that educational equality works against Black intermarriage. In this book, I re-examine this phenomenon by measuring the influence of educational equality on interracial identification incidence. Consistent with interracial marriage studies in which cities with more highly educated Black groups have higher monoracial marriage incidence, I find that cities with more highly educated

Black groups also have higher monoracial identification incidence. Black-Asians are no exception; the more Blacks are proportionately educated at the same levels as Asians, the more likely Blacks are to identify as monoracially Black. This means that racial equality between Blacks and Asians works against interracial identification incidence among Blacks, just as racial equality has been found to work against Black interracial marriage in the marriage demography literature.

Similarly, the more Asians are proportionately educated at the same levels as Blacks, the more likely Asians are to identify as monoracially Asian. The multivariate coefficient for measuring the influence of educational equality in the Black-Asian model is considerably greater than that in the Asian-Black model. This suggests that educational equality between the two racial groups is less likely to encourage Blacks to identify as half Asian than it is to encourage Asians to identify as half Black. This indicates that educational equality between Blacks and Asians impacts Blacks more than it does Asians. In summary, my analyses find that educational equality between Blacks and Asians decreases biracial identification incidence between them, and it decreases biracial identification incidence among Blacks more than it does among Asians.

Finally, let's discuss how relative racial group size influences biracial identification incidence. The theory holds that members of smaller groups will be more likely to have intergroup relations because the small group size numerically reduces the size of the in-group selection pool, and because members of smaller group are more likely to be more distributed across different social circles that overlap with the out-group. In smaller groups, members will be more challenged to find similar-status others within their own racial group. In larger groups, the opposite is true; members of larger racial groups will have a good-sized selection pool of same-status, same-race mate options to choose from, and according to the theory, will be more likely to form relationships with these same-race peers than they will be to form interracial relationships.

Marriage demographers have found that larger groups are less likely to intermarry and smaller groups are more likely to intermarry. As a whole, Blacks are a much larger group than Asians, making national interracial marriage less numerically probable for Blacks than for Asians. In this book, I re-examine this phenomenon by measuring the influence of relative group size on interracial identification incidence. Consistent with interracial marriage studies in which cities with larger Black groups have lower interracial marriage incidence, I find that cities with larger Black groups also have lower interracial identification incidence, and Black-Asians are no exception. The larger the Black group size relative to the Asian group size, the less likely Blacks are to identify as biracially Asian, even after residential segregation and educational equality are taken into account. This means that group size works against interracial identification incidence among Blacks, just as group size has been found to work against Black interracial marriage in the marriage demography literature.

Meanwhile, Asians as a whole are a much smaller group than Blacks, making interracial marriage more probable for Asians than for Blacks (Fu and Heaton 2000; Heaton and Jacobson 2000; Hwang et al. 1994; Kalmijn and Van Tubergen 2010; Qian 1999). Consistent with interracial marriage studies in which cities with smaller Asian groups have higher interracial marriage incidence, I find that cities with smaller Asian groups also have higher interracial identification incidence, and Asian-Blacks are no exception. The smaller the Asian group size relative to the Black group size, the more likely Asians are to identify as biracially Black, even after residential segregation and educational equality are taken into account. This means that group size favors interracial identification incidence among Asians, just as group size has been found to favor Asian interracial marriage in the marriage demography literature. Both Blacks and Asians are less likely to identify interracially with one another as their preferred monoracial group grows larger, which is consistent with the theory and intermarriage empiricism on other racial pairings.

The Asian racial group in the United States is growing much faster than the Black racial group due to immigration (Edmonston et al. 2002; Hoeffel et al. 2012). Immigration interacts with group size, as well as segregation and education. Educated immigrants, as well as Blacks and Asians who immigrate to seek higher education in the United States, are less likely to reside in segregated neighborhoods. Instead they seek the diverse neighborhoods that surround educational institutions. Meanwhile, less educated Black and Asian immigrants not pursing higher education often seek ethnic enclaves in the destination. Black ethnic enclaves are a way for Black immigrants to set themselves apart from Americans-born Blacks (Waters 1999), which is not the same dynamic for Asians. Asian immigration actually increases the same-race marriage pool for American-born Asians (Lichter and Qian 2005). Asian immigrants are therefore more likely to marry other Asians in the United States than they are to marry outside their race (Hwang et al. 1994; Lee and Fernandez 1998; Lichter and Qian 2005; Qian 1999; Tafoya 2002). In this study, I find no statistically significant relationship between group-level Asian nativity and Asian biracial identification incidence with Blacks across cities. But I do find a small, statistically significant relationship for Blacks; the greater the percentage of Blacks that are foreign-born in a given city, the greater the Black-Asian biracial identification incidence in that city.

This book is about the geographic variation in biracial identification incidence across cities, what structural dynamics are at play in these cities that can explain that variation, and how these structural dynamics influence different biracial groups differently in their likelihood to claim biracial identification. Part of a city's culture, and importantly, its racial tone, is a function of the historical relationship between different racial groups in that city's region. Whereas the Black-White divide in the South encourages Black monoracial reporting (Blum 1984; Harris and Sim 2002), the history of Asian discrimination in the West does not likewise encourage Asian monoracial reporting (JACL 2008; Kitano et al. 1984). That is, the percentage of Blacks in the South that interracially identify with Whites is much smaller than chance would expect, while the percentage of Asians in the West that interracially identify with Whites is not smaller than chance would expect. And even though the culture and social structure in the South discourages Black-White interracial identification, there are still more biracial Black-Whites in the South than any other census region. Of all the biracial Black-Whites, a third live in the South. But Blacks in the South are not necessarily more likely to identify with Asians than they are in other regions once the effects of residential segregation, educational equality, group size, and nativity are taken into account. Meanwhile, nearly half of all biracial Asian-Whites reside in the West. Yet, this chapter finds that Asians are less likely to identify as partially Black in the West compared to other regions once these other structural factors are taken into account.

Overall, I find that Asian Americans claim interracial identification more often than Blacks, just as Asians interracially marry more often than Blacks. Interracial marriage for each racial group is threatened by different rates of marital stability (Zhang and Vanhook 2009) and cohabitation in place of marriage (Lichter and Qian 2005; Qian et al. 2012). Asian interracial marriage incidence is expected to slow as segregation, educational attainment, group size, and immigration trends change (Lee and Fernandez 1998; Lichter and Qian 2005). In contrast, Asian interracial identification is expected to grow (Edmonston et al. 2002). This is true especially as Asian Americans continue to be seen as "foreign," and they respond by putting more emphasis on a desire to project an American-citizen master status (Williams 1992, Williams and Thornton 1998). Given trends in interracial marriage, trends in interracial identification, and findings from the analyses in this book, there is support for further focus on interracial identification over interracial marriage as we continue to seek an understanding of interracial relations in America.

This study borrows from Peter Blau's macrostructural theory on intergroup relations and subsequent empirical scholarship on interracial marriage to assess the effects of macrostructural variables on the likelihood of Blacks and Asians reporting biracial identification with one another in the 2010 U.S. Census. By evaluating the extent social forces known to influence interracial marriage also influence interracial identification, I have extended Blau's theory beyond explaining the likelihood two different-race people will marry, to the likelihood one person will identify with two different races. Blau's theory depends on the comparison of two groups in which one is a minority and the other is a majority. The theory lends itself to "race" as the demographic characteristic defining group membership, and empirical studies testing the theory consistently choose Whites as the majority group and either Blacks, Asians, or Hispanics as the minority group. This chapter assesses the applicability of Blau's macrostructural theory of intergroup relations when two non-White racial groups are at hand, Blacks and Asians, to better understand inter-minority dynamics.

This book contrasts the meaning of "minority" as Blau intended (numerically), with the idea of "minority" defined by oppression. Whereas the Asian-Black model in this chapter positions Asians as the minority, the Black-Asian model positions Blacks as the minority. As shown by the respective R^2 values, the two models have fairly similar strength, with the Black-Asian model strength 5.9 percentage points stronger than the Asian-Black model. These models are stronger than the Asian-White model described in chapter 3 ($R^2 = 61.1$ percent) but considerably weaker than the Black-White model described in chapter 2 ($R^2 = 91.1$ percent).

Blau's theory explains the likelihood of intergroup relations and therefore rests on the assumption that there is some degree of social distance between the two groups. (If the two groups lacked social distance, there would be no sociological phenomenon worth explaining because relationships among members from the two groups would not be noteworthy.) As such, the extent to which the theory accounts for two groups coming together arguably alludes to the extent to which the two groups stand apart from one another. Under this line of reasoning, the stronger the R^2 of each model, the greater the social distance between the two racial groups incorporated into each model.

Of the four models tested (i.e., Black-White in chapter 2, Asian-White in chapter 3, and Asian-Black and Black-Asian both in this chapter), the Black-White model in chapter 2 is by far the strongest ($R^2 = 91.1$ percent) and the Asian-White model in chapter 3, although still fairly strong for the social sciences, is the weakest ($R^2 = 61.1$ percent). This indicates that Blacks have more social distance with Whites than Asians have with Whites, which is consistent with countless studies concluding that Blacks remain at the bottom of the American racial hierarchy (Bean and Stevens 2003; Bratter 2007; Gans 2007; Lee and Bean 2004, 2007a, 2007b; Lichter and Qian 2005; Qian 1997).

Blau's theory rests on the foundation that one group is a minority and the other a majority. In most cases, Whites are both the numerical and the cultural majority. But when two non-White groups are modeled together, it begs the question of which group plays the role of the minority and which plays the role of the majority. Blau does not explicitly specify in his theory whether the minority group is defined by numerical proportion or by historical oppression. The models testing his theory are almost unanimously White versus minority, so the minority group is both the numerical minority and the oppressed group. Macrostructural scholars, however, by the nature of their work, would likely define minority as numerical if forced to choose. And since they consistently test Blau's theory with Whites acting as the majority group, it is quite possible this definition has not been challenged in the past. Tested both ways, first positioning Asians as the minority group and then positioning Blacks as the minority group, the stronger R^2 in the Black-Asian model suggests that the effect of Blacks as an oppressed minority trumps the effect of Asians as a numerical minority.

This chapter again confirms that Blau's theory of intergroup relations, most commonly applied to the context of interracial marriage, applies very well to interracial identification. I find that interracial identification can be explained by macrostructural factors, a line of inquiry that has not received attention from macrostructural demographers or interracial identification scholars previously. Also previously under-considered, I test non-White, inter-minority models to pick apart the meaning of minority defined numerically versus the reality of minority defined by oppression. By simultaneously deploying four different models at once over the course of this book (i.e., Black-White in chapter 2, Asian-White in chapter 3, and Asian-Black and Black-Asian both in this chapter), I'm able to build upon both the macrostructural literature and the racial identification body of knowledge through a dialogue of compare-and-contrast, which I continue into the next chapter.

NOTES

1. For each city, the number of Blacks and Asians reporting monoracial and biracial identification with each other (and with Whites) is available from Census Summary File 1.

2. Due to a number of factors, I expect to see many more published studies in this area very soon (Venkatraman and Lockhart 2020; Washington 2017).

3. As a dummy variable, region cannot be transformed because $\ln(0)$ is undefined.

4. Nine metropolitan areas have percentages greater than three standard deviations (means of 5.0 percent or greater). All these are in the South.

5. Eleven metropolitan areas have percentages greater than three standard deviations (means of 2.2 percent or greater). All these are in the West.

Conclusion

Guess Who's Coming to Dinner Now

This book examines how different social structure elements affect the likelihood racial minority groups identify as biracial, despite the fact that American social norms tend to lead multiracial people to identify monoracially. As many as three in four Blacks are believed to be multiracial according to Davis (1991), yet because social norms overwhelmingly categorize these folks as "just-Black," a relatively small proportion of Blacks self-identify with more than one race on the census. Therefore, the degree to which racial minorities breech this norm by identifying biracially says something about the environment in which they live, and importantly, the degree of social distance between different racial groups.

To assess how different structural factors in urban environments influence the proportion of racial minority groups choosing to identify biracially, I leverage theory focused on explaining social structure's influence on intergroup relations. I review accompanying empiricism confirming the theory's postulates on the application of interracial marriage. And I then extend the theory to the application of interracial identification. With interracial marriage less stable (and less likely in the first place) compared to same-race couples, I propose interracial *people* replace interracial *marriage* as the new preferred macrostructural indicator of racial distance.

In my discussions, I fold in qualitative findings from racial identity scholars, and quantitative findings from multiracial identification scholars focused on micro- and meso-level characteristics to explain macro-level findings from each of four tests detailed in this book. I also compare and contrast how and why environmental factors affect different racial groups in different ways at the macrostructural level, and what that says about social distance between racial groups.

STRUCTURAL DETERMINANTS OF
INTERGROUP RELATIONS

The tests executed in this book were directed by a theoretical framework set forth to explain intergroup relations. There are three main theories of intergroup relations: Exchange theory (Homans 1958), assimilation theory (Gordon 1964; Park 1926), and opportunity-structure theory (Simmel 1908). Exchange and assimilation theories have been criticized as Anglo-conformist and over-reliant on economic motivations (Bean and Stevens 2003; Blau 1994). Opportunity structure theory, alternatively, is believed to wield a greater degree of influence on social life than micro- and meso-level approaches (Blau 1977). This paper utilizes opportunity structure theory as developed by Peter Blau.

Opportunity structure theory starts with the assumption that people prefer relationships with those in their own group.[1] Simmel (1908) says that relationships can happen between people from different groups if they are similar in many other ways. Blau (1977) agrees with Simmel and adds that the degree to which different racial groups have anything in common is dictated by certain structural factors. Blau's development of opportunity structure theory, called macrostructural theory, presents a framework for evaluating the influence of multiple structural factors on the likelihood of intergroup relations.

Again, the basic premise of the theory starts with people preferring relationships with members of their own group. However, there are certain macro-level conditions that increase the likelihood people will go outside their group for relationships. In its simplest form, exposure to the other group, equality between the two groups, and group size relative to the other group influences whether people will be more likely to have relations outside their group. These structural elements determine the likelihood of intergroup relations. In the macrostructural interracial marriage literature, they are often referred to as *structural determinants* of intergroup relations.

GUESS WHO'S COMING TO DINNER

Blau's macrostructural theory was published in 1977. He tested it on interracial marriage in 1984 and retested it with different scholars in different ways from 1984 to 1988. As is custom in any theory development process, Blau and colleagues' tests evaluated the theory itself, in addition to evaluating whether interracial marriage was a valid operationalization of the theory. For the decade that followed, various empiricists tested it further, largely applying it to interracial marriage. Armed with findings and recommendations from many high-quality tests, Blau come out with a revision in 1994 offering a more parsimonious model for testing the theory. Much more empiricism followed, but has waned in recent years. This is likely due to saturation from consistently supported findings, coupled with a limited number of racial groups to test.

Intermarriage has by far been the most common application of intergroup relations tested under Blau's framework. Why is it important to study interracial relationships? Because it says something about the social distance between racial groups (Fu and Heaton 1997; Kalmijn 1998; Kalmijn and Van Tubergen 2010; Lee and Bean 2004; Lichter and Qian 2005; Qian, Glick and Batson 2012; Suro 1999; Zhang and Vanhook 2009). For example, if marriages between Blacks and Whites were on the rise, this would suggest the social distance between them was decreasing. In the theory's hay-day, intermarriage was considered the most prolonged type of intergroup relation (with interracial friendship, cohabitation, and crime as alternative applications).

But today, that may not be the case. Multiple scholars have suggested racial identification might be a more suitable social distance indicator for today's society (Bean and Stevens 2003; Bratter 2007; Lee and Bean 2004; Kalmijn 1993). However, no one has yet extended Blau's theory of intergroup relations and the accompanying empiricism on interracial marriage to the application of interracial identification.

GUESS WHO'S COMING TO DINNER *NOW*

This book resurrects Blau's theory, repurposing it from explaining the likelihood persons from two different races will marry, to the likelihood a person will identify with two different races. If structural factors influence interracial relations, and intermarriage begets interracial population, then do the same factors affecting intermarriage affect interracial identification? If so, do these factors affect different racial groups differently? And if so, why?

For the first time in U.S. history, Census 2000 respondents were allowed to choose more than one racial category. Over 6 million took advantage of this option by identifying with two races. By the 2010 Census, this biracial incidence figure grew over 30 percent, despite total American population growth of only about 10 percent. Either interracial parents are producing three times the number of offspring as the general population, or survey respondents are feeling more liberated to breech the age-old social norm pressuring multiracial people to identify monoracially. Notably, some racial groups are taking advantage of this option more than others. The ratio of Blacks to Whites is 0.18, suggesting that 18 percent of Blacks would be half White if race did not matter when choosing a partner or identifying one's self on a survey. But race does matter, and only 4.4 percent of Blacks say they are half White.

Conversely, the ratio of Asians to Whites is 0.08, suggesting that about 8 percent of Asian Americans would be half White, yet as many as 9.4 percent of Asians identified as such.

While these facts are at first blush intellectually interesting, the implications are much more than that. In this book, I present several relevant and unique contributions, which I'll summarize here.

Theoretical Extension

First, I asked whether the same macro-level factors influencing biracial marriage also influence biracial identification. The idea here is to present a case for theoretical extension. Why? Because many a respected scholar has regarded interracial marriage as a strong measure of racial distance and therefore an indication of America's social climate. Understanding the racial climate in the United States couldn't be any more important in the twenty-first century than it is at the time of this writing. The theory was wildly successful identifying and understanding the structures influencing interracial marriage. With marriage less stable (and less likely in the first place) among interracial couples, might interracial people present a more valid (and more stable) application of the theory? I tested whether interracial identification is a valid operationalization of the theory for the purpose of extending and reinvigorating a highly impactful social theory. All four analyses in this book provide very strong support for extending the theory beyond interracial marriage to the application of interracial identification .

Social Distance Indicators

The social distance between racial groups, known more concisely as racial distance, is an impact-laden topic with important implications for policy. Racial distance is a social construct. And like any social construct, it is operationalized (i.e., measured, captured, observed) through imperfect proxies. Any time social scientists try to size up something which cannot be directly measured in an exact way, we do the best we can by leveraging theory to guide us in finding suitable proxies that *can* be directly measured. We then test the proxy's suitability again and again, often refining how we capture that proxy in order to better reflect the underlying, not directly measurable, social construct. Per the theory, intergroup relations serve as a proxy for social distance. Within the context of race, interracial relations serve as a proxy for racial distance. Interracial relations have been extensively observed, measured, and tested through interracial marriage incidence figures for many decades. That is, interracial marriage is an observable and measurable proxy for racial distance. But whereas interracial marriage has been a popular racial distance indicator in the past, I now propose interracial identification begin to take its place.

Marriage isn't exactly the stable institution that it once was, even among same-race couples. And although the literature argues that racial identity is also not stable, the instability of racial identity actually works in favor of the argument I present here: *when more people identify with more than one race* (whether the source is increased birthrates from interracial couples or more multiracial people transitioning away from a lean toward monoracial identification), *this suggests less social distance between those races.* Racial identity is indeed fluid; it is situational and contextual, and changes over the life course. But the degrees to which multiracial people wax and wane on whether to identify as monoracial or multiracial still indicates social distance.

With a theoretical extension to Blau's framework confirmed in this book, my second contribution proposes substituting interracial marriage with interracial identification as the preferred macrostructural racial distance indicator. I substantiate this proposal with the analyses in this book yielding stronger R^2s using interracial identification incidence as the dependent variable than studies using interracial marriage incidence as the dependent variable, where comparable (i.e., largely macrostructural interracial marriage studies focused on Blacks and Whites).

Beyond Black and White

Much like empiricism on biracial marriage and other forms of interracial relations, biracial identification empiricism gravitates toward the Black-White divide. The convenience of strong sample size aside, Blacks and Whites are studied together for many important reasons. Blacks and Whites are more socially, culturally, and spatially distant than any other racial pairing. Residential segregation, inequality, and other indicators of oppression stand between Blacks and Whites more than any other two racial groups in the United States. Blacks are the least likely group to identify biracially with Whites (per a quick look at census counts), despite being more likely to share heritage with Whites than any other racial group (per Davis 1991 and others). Today, Blacks are disproportionately being restrained, beaten, and dying at the hands of police officers who are rarely brought to justice. Often these police officers are White, but many times they are not. Nonetheless, the police system is subjected to, and is a reflection of, a system that maintains White supremacy over Blacks. (See Coats, 2015 and Oluo, 2018 for powerful discussions of police brutality against Blacks.) Police brutality is but one of many symptoms of a deeper plague between Blacks and Whites, and every one of us is symptomatic. Perhaps the greatest of American tragedies is the persistent effect of slavery on contemporary American culture—a curse from which we may never fully recover. These and other factors make interracial relations between Blacks and Whites a popular and important topic among sociologists, psychologists, criminologists, and public policy makers.

Meanwhile, other racial pairings receive much less attention. In my experience teaching courses on race and ethnicity, and social problems, I'm always surprised by how many young adults arrive at university completely unaware of the history of Asian discrimination and racism in America, especially the tragedies inflicted during World War II right here on American soil. Many Asians have been subjected to forced internment camps, property seizures based purely on race alone, and continued mainstream media ridicule. They actually face more employment discrimination, issues voting, and lack political representation, despite the guise of the "model minority" myth (JACL 2008). Asian Americans are perceived as "foreigners" threatening our economy, culture, and our health. They've been blamed and publicly shamed for illogical presumptions that, by association, they present a threat to American public health and safety after various infectious diseases originating in Asian countries made their way to American cities. Examples of global, deadly epidemics include the Asian Flu (1956), Hong Kong Flu (1968), SARS (2002), various bird flus such as H5N1 (1997, 2012, 2013), and most recently, the COVID-19 "coronavirus" (2019). Labels (e.g., "Chinese Virus") that have been introduced into American public discourse by prominent public officials have coincided with an onslaught of Asian Americans being spit on, yelled at, and fatally attacked in recent times. At the time of this writing, these incidences are being reported on an almost daily basis. Chinese Americans are fearing for their safety. Similar experiences have been common over the past century, whether the association was with a pandemic, a world war, or various forms of government such as communism. Often Asians experience hate crimes based simply on "how they look." That said, three analyses in this book substantiate the choice to examine racial distance between other biracial groups beyond Black-White, representing the third contribution of this text.

Comparative Design

It is peculiar that nearly as many Asians as Blacks identified as half White on the 2010 Census, even though the total Asian American population is 2.4 times smaller number than the total Black population. Whereas Asians total 17.3 million, 1.6 million identified as biracially White. Meanwhile Blacks total 42.0 million, and 1.8 million identified as biracially White. Knowing that biracial identification is affected by the current racial climate and its effects, the degree to which structural factors affect Blacks differently than Asians has implications for policy. However there is a shortage of macrostructural empiricism comparing and contrasting the outcomes of different groups. To really do this effectively, the analytic design must include multiple racial pairings simultaneously in the same study. This presents an opportunity for the book to make a fourth contribution.

To be able to effectively compare and contrast the outcomes of different groups in a way in which findings influencing policy can be derived, I incorporated design-of-experiment (DOE) principles. Unlike studies in the past that have focused on minority/White pairs or minority/all-others-combined, I was careful to set up my analytic design with isolated cells. By including Black-White, Asian-White, Asian-Black, and Black-Asian groups in my study, I can compare Blacks and Asians, as well as isolate the relevance of Whiteness from the broader relevance of biracial categorization.

I suspect the lean toward Black and White, and the separate and smaller lean toward Asian and White, is to some degree a reflection of academia itself. I'll be bold here and say that my own observation has been that academics in the social sciences overwhelmingly specialize in studying themselves. It's fairly rare, for example, that I see Black scholars publishing work about Asian racial issues, or male sociologists focused on closing the gender gap. There are exceptions, of course, but the point I'm trying to make here is that we are in desperate need of more intersection. Studies that replicate a single analytic design on multiple racial groups enable apples-to-apples comparisons across racial groups existing in a multi-tiered racial hierarchy that is the United States of America. By simultaneously comparing and contrasting how four different racial pairings are influenced by the same macrostructural factors differently, I take a step toward closing that gap.

Inter-Minority Dynamics

I test Blacks and Whites to evaluate whether Blau's theoretical framework can be extended. Additionally, Blacks and Whites are two racial groups in the United States with the greatest social distance, and I wanted to be able to compare my interracial identification model strength to that of comparable interracial marriage models, as improved model strength would support using biracial identification incidence over biracial marriage incidence as a "new and improved" social distance indicator. I test the model on Asian-Whites because neither a theoretical extension nor a change in social distance indicators would be appropriate if the connection only applied to one racial group and not another. I also test an Asian-White model because racism against Asians is often underestimated. Finally, the Asian-White model provides a relative benchmark to put the Black-White model into perspective, and the findings hinted at a multi-tiered racial hierarchy, as opposed to a dichotomous social structure as some scholars have argued.

The fifth contribution of this book is to complete the White, Black, and Asian trifecta with double-minority models including both Blacks and Asians to better understand inter-minority dynamics. Neither the macrostructural literature on interracial marriage nor the quantitative racial identification literature looking at micro- and meso-level influences on identity have given inter-minority dynamics attention. By comparing the percentage of Asians identifying as half Black to the percentage of Blacks identifying as half Asian, and then comparing these models to the Black-White and Asian-White models, I find further confirmation of a multi-tiered racial hierarchy model. Incorporating this purview into the analysis allowed me to unpack the meaning of *minority* as numerically defined, versus a meaning and experience that is driven by oppression.

Macro-Level Dynamics Influencing Racial Identification

The sixth contribution of this book is that it presents a methodological extension of our understanding of racial identification by folding in a fully macro-level perspective. Racial identification has been extensively examined at the micro- and meso-levels. Family composition, education, skin tone, social network composition, experiences, memories, religion, politics, news, art, social movement, culture, and so on all impact whether an individual chooses to identify biracially. Meanwhile, this study finds that macro-level, structural dynamics like residential segregation, inequality in educational attainment, relative group size, nativity incidence, and geographic region substantially impact the likelihood of biracial identification incidence across cities. Many biracial identification studies have included a macrostructural variable or two in meso-level analyses, but this work is aimed at understanding variation between individuals (and sometimes groups) in the likelihood to identify biracially. None has deployed a fully macrostructural model aimed at understanding the drastic geographic variation in biracial identification incidence—until now. Building upon individual-level, household-level, and group-level analyses, this book presents the first city-level biracial identification analysis of its kind. Together with micro- and meso-level work from other scholars investigating what factors influence interracial identification, the macro-level forces identified in this book provide a perspective on racial identification at a new altitude.

TRANSCENDING INTERRACIAL MARRIAGE: INTERRACIAL IDENTIFICATION

Theory portends that the likelihood of intermarriage is subject to structural factors that can interfere with relationship opportunities. First, cities[2] where the minority group has greater exposure to the majority group have higher incidence of intergroup relations. The equivalent of this theorem, repurposed to explain biracial identification incidence is: the more minorities are exposed to the majority group, the more minorities report biracial identification with the majority group. Second, cities with greater equality between groups have lower likelihoods of intergroup relations. In terms of biracial identification likelihood, this means the greater the educational equality between two racial groups, the more minorities report monoracial identification. Finally, cities with smaller minority groups have higher incidence of intergroup relations. Similarly, the smaller the minority group relative to the majority group, the more minorities report biracial identification with the majority group.

Biracial identification incidence is the dependent variable in the study. This is the percentage of the minority group identifying as also of a majority group racial heritage, or the percentage of Race A identifying as also Race B. The first independent variable is minority exposure to the majority group, which I measure using the exposure index of segregation. That is, the average percent of an area that is White within the neighborhood of a Black person, for example. The second independent variable is equality between groups. I use education rather than income to measure equality because income is volatile. I measure educational equality with the inverse of the chi-square statistic. The independence between race and education is interpreted as educational equality between two racial groups. The third independent variable is minority group size relative to the majority group, or more specifically, the number of all Race A members per 1,000 monoracial Race B members. I control for the percentage of each minority group foreign-born. I also account for geographic region, controlling the South when Blacks are positioned as the racial minority group, and the West when Asians are positioned as the racial minority group.

Nearly all constructs in the theory depend on positioning one group as the minority group, and the other group as the majority group. In the past, Blau did not specify in his theory or empiricism any guidelines for testing a model excluding Whites. I test the percentage of Blacks half White and the percent of Asians half White. Further, when I test Asian-Black biracials, I test it both ways—first positioning Asians as the minority (numerical minority), and then positioning Blacks as the minority (as defined by prolonged oppression).

GROUP DIFFERENCES YIELD NEW INSIGHTS

The two models explaining the likelihood of minority groups identifying as partly White are similar in some ways and different in others. Group size is the strongest explanatory measure in both models. The percentage of Black identifying as partly White increases 0.4 percent and .2 percent for every 1 percent decrease in Black and Asian group size, respectively, relative to Whites. The second strongest explanatory measure in both models is exposure. The percentage of Blacks identifying as also White increases 0.7 percent for every 1 percent increase in Black exposure to Whites. The percentage of Asians identifying as also White increases 0.3 percent for every 1 percent increase in Asian exposure to Whites. In both models, equality is the third strongest predictor. The percent of Blacks identifying as half White decreases 0.07 percent for every 1 percent increase in Black-White equality. The percent of Asians identifying as half White decreases 0.1 percent for every 1 percent increase in Asian-White equality. The notable difference is that the Black-White model has the strongest R^2 of all four models, and the Asian-White model, although still strong, has the weakest.

To test the influence of structural factors on the likelihood Asians and Blacks identify biracially with one another, I had to create two models—one with Asians positioned as the minority, which they are, numerically, and the other with Blacks positioned as the minority, which they are, in terms of prolonged oppression. These two models performed quite similarly. The adjusted values of the R^2 values are similar, with the Black-Asian model slightly stronger than the Asian-Black model. As with the White biracial models, group size is again the strongest predictor. The percent of Asians who are also Black increases 0.3 percent for every 1 percent decrease in Asian group size, relative to Blacks. The percent of Blacks who are also Asian increases 0.5 percent for every 1 percent decrease in Black group size, relative to Asians. Again, exposure increases biracial identification, while equality decreases it. Exposure seems to be slightly more relevant to Asians identifying as half Black, while equality seems to be slightly more relevant to the likelihood Blacks identify as half Asian. Conclusively, all four models provide overall support for this new application of Blau's theory.

IN CLOSING

This study contributes to our understanding of race in America in several ways. First, it extends Peter Blau's macrostructural theory to an entirely different type of interracial phenomenon. Blau's (1977) theory explained interrelations. Blau's colleagues repeatedly tested the theory on *intermarriage*. This book tests the theory on *interidentification*. Indeed, all four analyses in this book provide very strong support for extending the theory beyond intergroup relations (and intermarriage in particular) to the application of interidentification.

Second, this study seizes the opportunity to take advantage of newly established data to examine the suitability of biracial identification as a social distance indicator for today's society. In fact, I propose substituting intermarriage with interidentification as the preferred macrostructural indicator of racial distance. I substantiate this proposal by finding stronger R^2 with interracial identification incidence as the dependent variable than comparable studies from the past have found with interracial marriage incidence as the dependent variable.

Neither a theoretical extension nor a change in social distance indicators would be appropriate if the connection only applied to Blacks and Whites. This study adds to our understanding of interidentification by examining other racial pairings in addition to Blacks and Whites. Such a design helps inform policy protecting multiple racial groups. Importantly, this design is useful as a point of comparison to the Black-White test. The findings hinted at a multi-tiered racial hierarchy, as opposed to a dichotomous social structure some scholars have suggested. After three analyses beyond the Black-White model performed well, I present a perspective on the complexity of the racial structure in America.

Fourth, I fill a gap in the literature by replicating a single analytic design on multiple racial groups so that apples-to-apples comparisons can be made. This allowed me to see how different groups are influenced by the same macrostructural variables differently. Overall, findings support policy aimed at dismantling Black residential segregation and closing the gap on educational equality in order to close social distance gaps between racial groups.

One might argue that an analysis of race and identity using the imperfect science of survey methodology and discrete, categorical variables will never be able to capture the lived experience of racial identity. To some degree I might agree, as this study finds that the Black-White model and the Asian-White model are strikingly similar despite findings by Lou, Lalonde, and Wilson (2001) and Harris and Sim (2002) who contend that Black-Whites and Asian-Whites go through two totally different patterns of identity selection. Whereas it's true that structural analyses have been criticized for failing to acknowledge the cultural element, this study incorporates environmental factors that arguably capture cultural undertones. With Blacks, for example, the region variable accounts for some of the historical and political history with Whites, and the segregation variable likely accounts for some of the effect of hypodescents. With Asians, the nativity variable hints at a culture of interdependence and the need to seek an *American* master status, sometimes even more than a race-based master status. Importantly, this study finds Blacks experience the most social distance with Whites and Asians experience the least, aligning with more culture-focused approaches.

Such a design also allowed me to paint a picture of America's racial hierarchy. Much of the American racial structure discourse argues that our society is not made up of a racial hierarchy, but rather is simply bifurcated. While some scholars argue we live in a White/non-White society where group specification is irrelevant because of the overwhelming influence of the White ruling class, others argue we live in a Black/non-Black society where racial group doesn't really matter much (except in the case of Blacks, who are set apart from the opportunities afforded to the rest of society). By simultaneously comparing and contrasting how four different racial pairings are influenced by the same macrostructural factors differently, I certainly find evidence of a multi-tiered racial hierarchy.

Earlier chapters explain that the stronger the explanatory power of each model, the greater the social distance between groups. Whereas the Black-White model has the greatest R^2, the Asian-White model has the least. I find that Asians and Blacks have less social distance between them than Whites and Blacks do. But Asians and Blacks are more distant from one another than Asians and Whites. This suggests a racial hierarchy in which Whites are at the top, Blacks at the bottom, and Asians are in between, but not centered between the two. That is, the distance between Whites (at the top) and Asians (between Whites and Blacks) is shorter than the distance between Asians (between Whites and Blacks) and Blacks (at the bottom).

The fifth contribution of this book is a better understanding of inter-minority dynamics. I completed the trifecta between Blacks, Whites, and Asians by examining double-minority models including biracial Asians and Blacks. It's the first analysis of its kind to examine the applicability of Blau's theory of intergroup relations to two specified non-White racial groups in the United States with statistically significant results. It also fills a gap in the racial identification literature. By comparing the prevalence of Asians identifying as half Black to the prevalence of Blacks identifying as half Asian, and then comparing these models to the Black-White and Asian-White models, I find further evidence confirming a multi-tiered racial hierarchy model.

I deconstruct the meaning of "minority" by executing two double-minority models, one in which the group positioned as the minority is the numerical minority (Asians), and a second in which the group positioned as the minority is the more oppressed group (Blacks). The Black-Asian model is stronger than the Asian-Black model, suggesting Blacks experience more social distance from Asians than Asians experience social distance from Blacks. By contrasting the meaning of "minority" as numerical with the meaning of "minority" defined by prolonged oppression, I find that cultural oppression trumps group size when it comes to social distance from other groups and the disadvantages that that presents.

The sixth contribution of this book is that it provides a perspective on racial identification at a new altitude. This book presents the first city-level biracial identification analysis of its kind by deploying a fully macrostructural model aimed at understanding the drastic geographic variation in biracial identification incidence. Building upon individual- and group-level analyses published by other scholars aimed at understanding the individual variation in biracial identification, the city-level view presented in this book offers nuances previously under-discovered. This fully macro-level view complements biracial identification work performed at the micro- and meso-levels, providing a more complete picture of our understanding of racial identification in America.

NOTES

1. Note that groups can be defined on the basis of just about anything, but in the United States, the most defining group in society is arguably race.

2. Prior tests of Blau's theory (including the theory itself) recommend using metropolitan areas as the unit of analysis. Data show that the prevalence of biracial identification varies from city to city. Data at the metropolitan area level is available from the Census Bureau.

Appendix A

Preparatory Procedures

Procedures exercised in preparation for the analysis are outlined here. This includes a discussion of outliers, regression assumptions, transformations, and post-transformation regression diagnostics. There are several data requirements that must be met when using regression; not doing so calls into question the reliability and validity of regression as a suitable technique given the data. Before addressing each of these in turn, it is important to state that these requirements are applicable to both the individual variables as well as the modeled relationship as a whole (Hair et al. 2006).

OUTLIERS

Outliers are cases with unusual values given a particular variable or combination of multiple variables.

Univariate Outliers

Hair et al. (2006) recommends standardizing the values of each variable such that the mean is set to 0 and the standard deviation is set to 1. In data sets with sample sizes greater than 80, which is true for this analysis, cases with values greater than 4.0, or less than −4.0, are considered outliers. In the model with Blacks identifying as half White, there are two equality outliers, both in the South (i.e., Gainesville, Florida and Greenville, North Carolina). In the model with Asians identifying as also White, there is one segregation outlier (i.e., Laredo, Texas), three equality outliers (i.e., Trenton-Ewing, New Jersey; Lafayette, Indiana; and Columbus, Indiana), and five group size outliers, all in California (i.e., San Jose-Sunnyvale-Santa Clara; Stockton;

Los Angeles-Long Beach-Santa Ana; San Francisco-Oakland-Fremont; and Vallejo-Fairfield). In the model with Asians identifying as also Black, there are two biracial incidence outliers, both in the South (i.e., Sumter, South Carolina and Hinesville-Fort Stewart, Georgia) and three group size outliers (i.e., San Jose-Sunnyvale-Santa Clara, California; Corvallis, Oregon; and Wausau, Wisconsin). In the model with Blacks identifying as also Asian, there are several segregation outliers, all in California (i.e., San Jose-Sunnyvale-Santa Clara; San Francisco-Oakland-Fremont; Vallejo-Fairfield; Sacramento-Arden Arcade-Roseville; Napa; and Stockton) and a handful of group size outliers, all in the South (i.e., Danville, Virginia; Albany, Georgia; Pine Bluff, Arkansas; and Rocky Mount, North Carolina).

Outliers can be beneficial if they are actually "indicative of characteristics of the population that would not be discovered in the normal course of analysis" (Hair et al. 2006:73). In contrast, outliers are problematic if they are anomalies contradicting the characteristics that are consistent across all the other cases in the data set. Meanwhile, outliers are considered neutral if they are extreme cases (rather than anomalies) that *are* consistent with characteristics common in all other cases. The outliers described earlier are generally of this neutral variety.

However, there are some exceptions. For example, Asian education far exceeds Whites (in Trenton-Ewing, New Jersey; Lafayette, Indiana; and Columbus, Indiana, as stated). Columbus is the exception, as the other two are college towns. Another example: Asian group size far exceeds Blacks (in San Jose-Sunnyvale-Santa Clara, California; Corvallis, Oregon; and Wausau, Wisconsin). Due to an unusually heavy Hmong refugee immigration stream, Wausau is the exception. Methods scholars generally agree that outliers should not be omitted "unless demonstrable proof indicates that they are truly aberrant and not representative of any observations in the population" (Hair et al. 2006:76). While omission may improve subsequent regression models, it runs the risk of limiting the generalizability. I retain these two outliers for the sake of consistency across models.

Bivariate Outliers

In addition to the identification of outlying cases for each variable, outliers emerging from dependent-independent variable pairings must also be identified and assessed. These types of outliers can be problematic if both the x and the y are unusual (Fox 1991). Meanwhile, y-axis outliers that are generally near the mean of the x-axis, or in line with the x-axis, are considered relatively benign. There are some bivariate outliers evident in the data used in this book, but they are generally of the benign category.

REGRESSION ASSUMPTIONS

All the variables used as model inputs in this book were checked for linearity, independence of errors, homoscedasticity, and normality.

Linearity

A linear relationship between the dependent variable and each independent variable assures consistency in the data and accurate estimation of relationship strength. The most common way of testing for linearity is through the use of scatterplots (Hair et al. 2006). Scatterplots depicting curved data, rather than linear data, indicate problematic relationships. There is some evidence of curvature in the equality measure in the Black-White and Asian-Black models. Group size shows evidence of curvature in all four models.

Independence of Errors

Regression requires that error from model inputs cannot be correlated. This ensures that the relationships that emerge from the models are due to inputs rather than omissions. This assumption is most commonly violated in the data collection process or when using time series data (Hair et al. 2006). As such, identifying correlated errors at the univariate level is limited to investigating possible causes. Because this research uses census data referencing a single date in time, it is unlikely this assumption has been violated. Nonetheless, independence of errors was tested on the multivariate relationship (see appendix B).

Homoscedasticity

Equally distributed variance from the dependent variable across the range of each independent variable ensures hypothesis tests are neither too stringent nor too insensitive (Hair et al. 2006). Homoscedasticity can be tested visually with scatterplots of the dependent variable against each independent variable. Diamond- or coned-shaped distributions indicate heteroscedasticity. There is evidence of heteroscedasticity in multiple variables. Heteroscedasticity is often the result of normality violations.

Normality

A normal distribution of each variable assures validity in subsequent statistical tests (Hair et al. 2006). Normality can be tested visually with histograms, or with normal probability plots for a more reliable test. Statistical tests, such as a comparison of skewness and kurtosis estimates to the critical value of ±2.58 (.01 significance level), can also assess normality. Because normality is sensitive to sample size, data sets with less than 30 records, or more than 1,000, should be tested graphically and statistically. The sample size in this analysis is 363, so I examine skewness and kurtosis estimates statistically. There is some evidence of skewness in the Black exposure to Asian measure, as well as in all group size measures (except Blacks relative to Whites). Half of all variables also exhibit evidence of kurtosis.

TRANSFORMATIONS

Transformations can correct these types of data issues. As explained, different model inputs used in this book violate different regression assumptions. There are issues with normality, heteroscedasticity, and linearity. Fortunately, transformations correcting normality violations often correct other types of violations at the same time (Hair et al. 2006). As normality tests revealed, the data are plagued by positive skew with leptokurtic kurtosis (i.e., peaked, rather than flat). Hair et al. (2006) recommends log transformations for variables demonstrating positive skew sans platykurtic kurtosis (i.e., flat, rather than peaked). Log transformations are also recommended for data evidencing linearity problems where the curvature is shaped like the letter "c" tilted backward toward the intersection of the axes.

Theory may also suggest transformations given the nature of the data (Hair et al. 2006). Blau's (1994) theory suggests transforming all variables by taking the natural log for several reasons. Transforming variables helps statistical tests like OLS accommodate different-sized metropolitan areas, making WLS regression, or controlling for population size in OLS, unnecessary. Logged transformation also has the advantage of standardizing scales of different variables in order to aid in their comparison. Lastly, transformations circumvent the need for interaction terms because both log transformations and interaction terms produce multiplicative effects; the multiplicative effect from log transformations "leaves insufficient departures for the product term to correct" (Blau 1994:74). Blau (1994:76) argues interaction terms are unnecessary: "There is no advantage in substituting the use of product terms. Logarithmic transformations, multivariate intersection, and controlling possible other influences provide adequate procedures for testing the theorems."

Given the characteristics of the data and advice from the theorist, natural log transformations were performed on all variables[1] (except region[2]). Natural log is the power to which e would have to be raised to equal x. Once transformations were completed, transformed data were tested to determine whether the desired remedies were achieved. Normal probability plots suggest normality is generally achieved, possibly with the exception of one of the four exposure measures. Because three of the four exposure measures are repaired by log transformation, I chose not to further meddle with the remaining offender for the sake of model consistency, especially since both linearity and homoscedasticity were improved.

REGRESSION DIAGNOSTICS

As mentioned, regression requirements apply to both the individual variables, now corrected, and the modeled relationship as a whole. Once transformations were completed, these data met regression assumptions modeled at the multivariate level (see appendix B). Scatterplots of predicted values to observed values for each biracial combination group verify clear linearity. Scatterplots of residuals to observed values indicate independence of the errors. Scatterplots of residuals to predicted values indicate homoscedasticity. Normal P-P plots of observed values to expected values indicate normal distributions of errors.

Other Considerations

Multiple regression assumes that independent variables are somewhat related and therefore have to be isolated in order to assess the independent effects of each explanatory variable on the dependent variable. However, too much correlation between independent variables can be misleading in the interpretation of statistically significant results (Hair et al. 2006). Some degree of multicollinearity is inherent among structural variables (Blau 1994). Multicollinearity statistics performed on these data indicate that thresholds are not violated (see appendix B). In summary, post-transformational regression assumptions are not violated at the univariate or multivariate level, supporting the use of OLS regression.

NOTES

1. Transformations are typically only applied to independent variables unless heteroscedasticity is also an issue; heteroscedasticity requires the dependent variable to also be transformed (Hair et al. 2006).

2. As a dummy variable with values of 0 and 1, region cannot be transformed because $\ln(0)$ is undefined.

Appendix B

Regression Diagnostics

1. *Linearity*. The predicted values are linearly related to the observed values (post transformation).
2. *Independence* (of the errors; no serial correlation). Residuals do not appear to be linearly related to the dependent variable.
3. *Homoscedasticity* (constant variance of the errors versus the predictions). Residuals are not getting more spread out.
4. *Normality* (of the error distribution). The residuals are plotted close to the diagonal line.
5. *Multicollinearity*. Tolerance and the variance inflation factor (VIF) indicate multicollinearity thresholds are not violated.

References

Alvarez, Alvin N., Linda Juang, and Christopher T. H. Liang. 2006. "Asian Americans and Racism: When Bad Things Happen to 'Model Minorities'." *Cultural Diversity and Ethnic Minority Psychology* 12 (3):477–92.

Anderson, Robert N., and Rogelio Saenz. 1994. "Structural Determinants of Mexican American Intermarriage, 1975–1980." *Social Science Quarterly* 75 (2):414–30.

Arendt, Hannah. 1964. *Eichmann in Jerusalem: A Report on the Banality of Evil.* Harmondsworth, Middlesex: Penguin Books.

Banaji, Mahzarin R., and Anthony G. Greenwald. 2016. *Blind Spot: Hidden Biases of Good People.* New York: Bantam Books.

Bean, Frank D., and Gillian Stevens. 2003. *America's Newcomers and the Dynamics of Diversity.* The American Sociological Association's Rose Series in Sociology. New York: Russell Sage Foundation.

Berry, William D. 1993. *Understanding Regression Assumptions.* Series in Quantitative Applications in the Social Sciences, 92. Sage University Papers.

Blalock, Hubert M. 1967. *Toward a Theory of Minority Group Relations.* New York: John Wiley & Sons.

Blau, Judith R., and Peter M. Blau. 1982. "The Cost of Inequality: Metropolitan Structure and Violent Crime." *American Sociological Review* 47 (1):114–29.

Blau, Peter M. 1964. *Exchange and Power in Social Life.* New York: John Wiley & Sons, Inc.

———. 1977. *Inequality and Heterogeneity: A Primitive Theory of Social Structure.* New York: The Free Press.

———. 1980. "A Fable About Social Structure." *Social Forces* 58 (3):777–88.

———. 1994. *Structural Contexts of Opportunities.* Chicago: The University of Chicago Press.

Blau, Peter M., Carolyn Beeker, and Kevin M. Fitzpatrick. 1984. "Intersecting Social Affiliations and Intermarriage." *Social Forces* 62 (3):585–606.

Blau, Peter M., Terry C. Blum, and Joseph E. Schwartz. 1982. "Heterogeneity and Intermarriage." *American Sociological Review* 47 (1):45–62.

Blau, Peter M., and Joseph E. Schwartz. 1984. *Crosscutting Social Circles: Testing a Macrostructural Theory of Intergroup Relations.* Orlando: Academic Press.

Blum, Terry C. 1984. "Racial Inequality and Salience: An Examination of Blau's Theory of Social Structure." *Social Forces* 62 (3):607–17.

———. 1985. "Structural Constraints on Interpersonal Relations: A Test of Blau's Macrosociological Theory." *American Journal of Sociology* 91 (3):511–21.

Bratter, Jenifer. 2007. "Will 'Multiracial' Survive to the Next Generation? The Racial Classification of Children of Multiracial Parents." *Social Forces* 86 (2):821–49.

Broman, Clifford L., Harold W. Neighbors, and James S. Jackson. 1998. "Racial Group Identification Among Black Adults." *Social Forces* 67 (1):146–58.

Brown, J. Scott, Steven Hitlin, and Glen H. Elder Jr. 2006. "The Greater Complexity of Lived Race: An Extension of Harris and Sim." *Social Science Quarterly* 87 (2):411–31.

———. 2007. "The Importance of Being 'Other': A Natural Experiment About Lived Race Over Time." *Social Science Research* 36:159–74.

Brunsma, David L. 2005. "Interracial Families and the Racial Identification of Mixed-Race Children: Evidence from the Early Childhood Longitudinal Study." *Social Forces* 84 (2):1131–57.

———. 2006. "Public Categories, Private Identities: Exploring Regional Differences in the Biracial Experience." *Social Science Research* 35:555–76.

Butts, Rachel. 2008. "Guess Who's Coming to Dinner: Structural Determinants of Black-White Biracial Identification in the 2000 Census." MA Thesis, University of Oklahoma, Norman, OK.

———. 2009. "Guess Who's Coming to Dinner: Structural Determinants of Black-White Biracial Identification in the 2000 Census." Presented in the Structural Influences on Race/Ethnic Identification Division at the Annual Meeting of the Population Association of America, Detroit, MI.

Campbell, Mary E. 2007. "Thinking Outside the (Black) Box: Measuring Black and Multiracial Identification on Surveys." *Social Science Research* 36:921–44.

Castles, Stephen, and Mark J. Miller. 2003. *The Age of Migration: International Population Movements in the Modern World.* New York: Guilford Press.

Chideya, Farai. 1999. The Color of Our Future. New York: William Marrow and Company, Inc.

Coates, Ta-Nehisi. 2015. *Between the World and Me.* New York: Siegel & Grau.

Cortes, Dharma E., Sherry Deren, Jonny Andia, and Rafaela Robles. 2003. "The Use of the Puerto Rican Biculturality Scale with Puerto Rican Drug Users in New York and Puerto Rico." *Journal of Psychoactive Drugs* 35 (2):197–207.

Croll, Paul R. 2007. "Modeling Determinants of White Racial Identification: Results From a New National Survey." *Social Forces* 86 (2):613–41.

Davis, F. James. 1991. *Who is Black: One Nation's Definition.* University Park: Pennsylvania State University Press.

Dong, Yiran, and Chao-Ying Joanne Peng. 2013. "Principled Missing Data Methods for Researchers." *Springerplus* 2 (1):222.

Edmonston, Barry, Sharon M. Lee, and Jeffrey S. Passel. 2002. "Recent Trends in Intermarriage and Immigration and Their Effects on the Future Racial Composition of the US Population." In *The New Race Question: How the Census Counts Multiracial Individuals*, edited by Joel Perlmann and Mary C. Waters, 227–55. New York: Russell Sage Foundation.

Ellis, Lee. 1994. *Research Methods in the Social Sciences*. Madison: Brown & Benchmark.

Farley, Reynolds. 2002. "Racial Identities in 2000: The Response to the Multiple-Race Response Option." In *The New Race Question: How the Census Counts Multiracial Individuals*, edited by Joel Perlmann, and Mary C. Waters, 33–61. New York: Russell Sage Foundation.

———. 2011. "The Waning of American Apartheid?" *Contexts* (Summer):36–43.

Fischer, Mary J. 2003. "The Relative Importance of Income and Race in Determining Residential Outcomes in U.S. Urban Areas, 1970–2000." *Urban Affairs Review* 38 (5):669–96.

Fitzpatrick, Kevin M., and Sean-Shong Hwang. 1992. "The Effects of Community Structure on Opportunities for Interracial Contact: Extending Blau's Macrostructural Theory." *The Sociological Quarterly* 33 (1):51–61.

Fox, John. 1991. *Regression Diagnostics*. Series in Quantitative Applications in the Social Sciences, 79. Newbury Park: Sage University Papers.

Frey, William H. 2003. "Charticle." *The Milken Institute Review* (Third Quarter):7–10.

Frey, William H., and Reynolds Farley. 1996. "Latino, Asian, and Black Segregation in US Metropolitan Areas: Are Multiethnic Metros Different?" *Demography* 33 (1):35–50.

Fu, Xuanning, and Tim B. Heaton. 2000. "Status Exchange in Intermarriage Among Hawaiians, Japanese, Filipinos, and Caucasians in Hawaii: 1983–1994." *Journal of Comparative Family Studies* 31 (1):45–61.

Gans, Herbert J. 2007. "The Possibility of a New Racial Hierarchy in the Twenty-First Century United States." In *Rethinking the Color Line: Readings in Race and Ethnicity*. 3rd edition, edited by Charles A. Gallagher, 149–65. New York: McGraw-Hill.

Garza, Alicia, Patrisse Cullors, and Opan Tometi. n.d. "Black Lives Matter: About." Accessed October 13, 2020. https://Blacklivesmatter.com/about/.

Glesne, Corrine. 2006. *Becoming Qualitative Researchers: An Introduction*. 4th edition. Boston: Pearson Education, Inc.

Gordon, Milton M. 1964. *Assimilation in American Life: The Role of Race, Religion, and National Origins*. New York: Oxford University Press.

Hair Jr., Joseph F., William C. Black, Barry J. Babin, Rolph E. Anderson, and Ronald L. Tatham. 2006. *Multivariate Data Analysis*. 6th edition. Upper Saddle River: Pearson Prentice Hall.

Harris, David R. 2002. "Does It Matter How We Measure? Racial Classification and the Characteristics of Multiracial Youth." In *The New Race Question: How the Census Counts Multiracial Individuals*, edited by Joel Perlmann and Mary C. Waters, 62–101. New York: Russell Sage Foundation.

Harris, David R., and Jeremiah Joseph Sim. 2002. "Who is Multiracial? Assessing the Complexity of Lived Race." *American Sociological Review* 67 (4):614–27.

Heaton, Tim B., and Cardell K. Jacobson. 2000. "Intergroup Marriage: An Examination of Opportunity Structures." *Sociological Inquiry* 70 (1):30–41.

Hirschman, Charles. 2004. "The Origins and Demise of the Concept of Race." *Population and Development Review* 30 (3):385–415.

Hirschman, Charles, Richard Alba, and Reynolds Farley. 2000. "The Meaning and Measurement of Race in the US Census: Glimpses into the Future." *Demography* 37 (3):381–93.

Hitlin, Steven, J. Scott Brown, and Glen H. Elder Jr. 2006. "Racial Self-Categorization in Adolescence: Multiracial Development and Social Pathways." *Child Development* 77 (5):1298–1308.

———. 2007. "Measuring Latinos: Racial vs. Ethnic Classification and Self-Understandings." *Social Forces* 86 (2):587–611.

Hochschild, Jennifer L., and Vesla Weaver. 2007. "The Skin Color Paradox and the American Racial Order." *Social Forces* 86 (2):643–69.

Hoeffel, Elizabeth M., Sonya Rastogi, Myoung Ouk Kim, and Hasan Shahid. 2012. "The Asian Population: 2010." *2010 Census Briefs* (March):1–23.

Homans, George C. 1958. "Social Behavior as Exchange." *American Journal of Sociology* 63 (6):597–606.

Hutcheson, G. D. 2011. "Ordinary Least-Squares Regression." In *The Sage Dictionary of Quantitative Management Research*, edited by L. Moutinho and G. D. Hutcheson, 224–8. London: Sage.

Hwang, Sean-Shong, Rogelio Saenz, and Benigno E. Aguirre. 1994. "Structural and Individual Determinants of the Outmarriage Among Chinese-, Filipino-, and Japanese-Americans in California." *Sociological Inquiry* 64 (4):396–414.

———. 1997. "Structural and Assimilationist Explanations of Asian American Intermarriage." *Journal of Marriage and the Family* 59:758–72.

Japanese American Citizens League (JACL). 2008. *An Unnoticed Struggle: A Concise History of Asian American Civil Rights Issues.* San Francisco: JACL.

Justis, Rachel M. 2010. "Census 2010 Participation Rates." Indiana University Kelley School of Business, Indiana Business Research Center. Summer.

Kalmijn, Matthijs. 1993. "Trends in Black/White Intermarriage." *Social Forces* 72(1):119–46.

———. 1998. "Intermarriage and Homogamy: Causes, Patterns, Trends." *Annual Review of Sociology* 24:395–421.

Kalmijn, Matthijs, and Frank Van Tubergen. 2010. "A Comparative Perspective on Intermarriage: Explaining Differences Among National-Origin Groups in the United States." *Demography* 47 (2):459–79.

Kitano, Harry H. L., Wai-Tsang Yeung, Lynn Chai, and Herbert Hatanaka. 1984. "Asian-American Interracial Marriage." *Journal of Marriage and the Family* 179–90.

Knoke, David, George W. Bohrnstedt, and Alisa Potter Mee. 2002. *Statistics for Social Data Analysis.* 4th edition. Belmont: Thompson.

Lee, Jennifer, and Frank D. Bean. 2004. "America's Changing Color Lines: Immigration, Race/Ethnicity, and Multiracial Identification." *Annual Review of Sociology* 30:221–42.

———. 2007a. "Reinventing the Color Line: Immigration and America's New Racial/Ethnic Divide." *Social Forces* 86 (2):561–85.

———. 2007b. "Beyond Black and White: Remaking Race in America." In *Rethinking the Color Line: Readings in Race and Ethnicity.* 3rd edition, edited by Charles A. Gallagher, 122–9. New York: McGraw-Hill.

Lee, Sharon, and Marilyn Fernandez. 1998. "Trends in Asian American Racial/Ethnic Intermarriage." *Sociological Perspectives* 41 (2):323–42.

Lichter, Daniel T. 2013. "Integration or Fragmentation? Racial Diversity and the American Future." *Demography* 50:359–91.

Lichter, Daniel T., J. Brian Brown, Zhenchao Qian, and Julia H. Carmalt. 2007. "Marital Assimilation Among Hispanics: Evidence of Declining Cultural and Economic Indorporation?" *Social Science Quarterly* 88 (3):745–65.

Lichter, Daniel T., and Zhenchao Qian. 2005. "Marriage and Family in a Multiracial Society." In *The American People: Census 2000,* edited by Reynolds Farley and John Haaga, 169–200. New York: Russell Sage Foundation.

Lieberson, Stanley, and Mary C. Waters. 1985. "Ethnic Mixtures in the United States." *Sociology and Social Research* 70:43–52.

Liptak, Adam, and Michael Wines. 2020. "Supreme Court Rules That Census Count Can Be Cut Short." *New York Times,* October 13, 2020. https://www.nytimes.com /2020/10/13/us/supreme-court-census.html.

Lou, Evelina, Richard N. Lalonde, and Carlos Wilson. 2011. "Examining a Multidimensional Framework of Racial Identity Across Different Biracial Groups." *Asian American Journal of Psychology* 2 (2):79–90.

Loveman, Mara, and Jeronimo O. Muniz. 2007. "How Puerto Rico Became White: Boundary Dynamics and Intercensus Racial Reclassification." *American Sociological Review* 72 (6):915–39.

Mapping Police Violence. n.d. Accessed October 17, 2020. https://mappingpolicevi olence.org/.

Marsden, Peter V. 1990. "Network Diversity, Substructures, and Opportunities for Contact." In *Structures of Power and Constraint: Papers in Honor of Peter Blau,* edited by Craig Calhoun, Marshall W. Meyer, and W. Richard Scott, 397–410. Cambridge: Cambridge University Press.

Mass, Amy Iwasaki. 1992. "Interracial Japanese Americans: The Best of Both Worlds or the End of the Japanese American Community?" In *Racially Mixed People in America,* edited by Maria P. P. Root, 265–79. Newbury Park: Sage Publications.

Massey, Douglas S., and Nancy A. Denton. 1988. "The Dimensions of Residential Segregation." *Social Forces* 67 (2):281–315.

———. 1989. "Hypersegregation in U.S. Metropolitan Areas: Black and Hispanic Segregation along Five Dimensions." *Demography* 26 (3):373–91.

———. 1993. *American Apartheid: Segregation and the Making of the Underclass.* Cambridge: Harvard University Press.

Masuoka, Natalie. 2011. "The 'Multiracial' Option: Social Group Identity and Changing Patterns of Racial Categorization." *American Politics Research* 39 (1):176–204.

McPherson, Miller, Lynn Smith-Lovin, and James M. Cook. 2001. "Birds of a Feather: Homophily in Social Networks." *Annual Review of Sociology* 27 (1):415–44.

Messner, Steve F., and Scott J. South. 1986. "Economic Deprivation, Opportunity Structure, and Robbery Victimization: Intra- and Interracial Patterns." *Social Forces* 64 (4):975–91.

Oluo, Ijeoma. 2008. *So You Want to Talk About Race.* New York: Seal Press.

Park, Robert E. 1926. "Our Racial Frontier in The Pacific." *Survey Graphic* 9:192–96.

Park, Robert E., and Ernest W. Burgess. 1921. *Introduction to the Science of Sociology.* Chicago: University of Chicago Press.

Parker, J.D., N. Schenker, D.D. Ingram, J.A. Weed, K.E. Heck, and J.H. Madans. 2004. "Bridging Between Two Standards for Collecting Information on Race and Ethnicity: An Application to Census 2000 and Vital Rates." *Public Health Report* 119:192–205.

PayScale, n.d. "The Racial Wage Gap Persists in 2020." Accessed October 18, 2020. https://www.payscale.com/data/racial-wage-gap.

Peach, Ceri. 1980. "Ethnic Segregation and Intermarriage." *Annals of the Association of American Geographers* 70:371–81.

———. 1996. "Does Britain Have Ghettos?" *Transactions of the Institute of British Geographers* 21 (1):216–35.

Perlmann, Joel, and Mary C. Waters. 2002. "Introduction." *The New Race Question: How the Census Counts Multiracial Individuals*, edited by Joel Perlmann and Mary C. Waters, 1–30. New York: Russell Sage Foundation.

Population Studies Center. 2013. Exposure Indices. Ann Arbor: University of Michigan.

Qian, Zhenchao. 1997. "Breaking the Racial Barriers: Variations in Interracial Marriage Between 1980 and 1990." *Demography* 34 (2):263–76.

———. 1999. "Who Intermarries? Education, Nativity, Region, and Interracial Marriage, 1980 and 1990." *Journal of Comparative Family Studies* 30 (4):579–97.

Qian, Zhenchao, Jennifer E. Glick, and Christy D. Batson. 2012. "Crossing Boundaries: Nativity, Ethnicity, and Mate Selection." *Demography* 49 (2):651–75.

Renn, Kristen A. 2008. "Research on Biracial and Multiracial Identity Development: Overview and Synthesis." *New Directions for Student Services* 123:13–21.

Rockquemore, Kerry Ann, and David L. Brunsma. 2008. *Beyond Black: Biracial Identity in America.* New York: Rowman & Littlefield Publishers.

Root, Maria P. P. 1992. *Racially Mixed People in America.* Newbury: Sage Publications.

Roth, Wendy D. 2005. "The End of the One-Drop Rule? Labeling of Multiracial Children in Black Intermarriages." *Sociological Forum* 20 (1):35–67.

Rytina, Steven, Peter M. Blau, Terry Blum, and Joseph Schwartz. 1988. "Inequality and Intermarriage: A Paradox of Motive and Constraint." *Social Forces* 66 (3):645–75.

Sampson, Robert V. 1984. "Group Size, Heterogeneity, and Intergroup Conflict: A Test of Blau's Inequality and Heterogeneity." *Social Forces* 62 (3):619–39.

Saperstein, Aliya. 2006. "Double-Checking the Race Box: Examining Inconsistency Between Survey Measures of Observed and Self-Reported Race." *Social Forces* 85 (1):57–74.

Sassen, Saskia. 2001. *The Global City: New York, London, Tokyo.* Princeton: Princeton University Press.

———. 2006. *Territory, Authority, Rights: From Medieval to Global Assemblages.* Princeton: Princeton University Press.

Sassler, Sharon, and Kara Joyner. 2011. "Social Exchange and the Progression of Sexual Relationships in Emerging Adulthood." *Social Forces* 90 (1):223–46.

Schwartz, Joseph E. 1990. "Penetrating Differentiation: Linking Macro and Micro Phenomena." In *Structures of Power and Constraint: Papers in Honor of Peter Blau*, edited by Craig Calhoun, Marshall W. Meyer, and W. Richard Scott, 353–74. Cambridge: Cambridge University Press.

Simmel, Georg. [1908, 1922] 1955. *Conflict: The Web of Group Affiliations.* Translated by Reinhard Bendix. New York: The Free Press.

Skvoretz, John. 1983. "Salience, Heterogeneity, and Consolidation of Parameters: Civilizing Blau's Primitive Theory." *American Sociological Review* 48:360–75.

———. 1990. "Social Structure and Intermarriage: A Reanalysis." In *Structures of Power and Constraint: Papers in Honor of Peter Blau*, edited by Craig Calhoun, Marshall W. Meyer, and W. Richard Scott, 375–96. Cambridge: Cambridge University Press.

Song, Miri. 2003. *Choosing Ethnic Identity.* Malden: Polity Press.

South, Scott J., and Steven F. Messner. 1986. "Structural Determinants of Intergroup Association: Interracial Marriage and Crime." *The American Journal of Sociology* 91 (6):1409–30.

Spencer, John Michael. 1997. *The New Colored People: The Mixed-Race Movement in America.* New York: New York University Press.

St. John, Craig, and Robert Clymer. 2000. "Racial Residential Segregation by Level of Socioeconomic Status." *Social Science Quarterly* 81 (3):701–15.

Stanton, Jeffrey M. 2001. "Galton, Pearson, and the Peas: A Brief History of Linear Regression for Statistics Instructors." *Journal of Statistics Education* 9(3).

Stevens, Gillian, and Gray Swicewood. 1987. "The Linguistic Context of Ethnic Endogamy." *American Sociological Review* 52:73–82.

Suro, Roberto. 1999. "Mixed Doubles." *American Demographics* 21 (11):56–62.

Tafoya, Sonya M. 2002. "Mixed Race and Ethnicity in California." In *The New Race Question: How the Census Counts Multiracial Individuals*, edited by Joel Perlmann and Mary C. Waters, 102–15. New York: Russell Sage Foundation.

Tafoya, Sonya M., Hans Johnson, and Laura E. Hill. 2005. "Who Chooses to Choose Two?" In *The American People: Census 2000*, edited by Reynolds Farley and John Haaga, 332–51. New York: Russell Sage Foundation.

Townsend, Sarah S. M., Stephanie A. Fryberg, Clara L. Wilkins, and Hazel Rose Markus. 2012. "Being Mixed: Who Claims a Biracial Identity?" *Cultural Diversity and Ethnic Minority Psychology* 18 (1):91–6.

Tucker, M. Belinda, and Claudia Mitchell-Kernan. 1990. "New Trends in Black American Interracial Marriage: The Social Structural Context." *Journal of Marriage and the Family* 52 (1):209–18.

US Census Bureau. 2008. "A Compass for Understanding and Using American Community Survey Data: What General Data Users Need to Know." Washington DC: US Government Printing Office.

———. 2009. "American Community Survey Fundamentals." Presented at the annual meeting of the Population Association of America, Detroit, MI.

———. 2010. "Strength in Numbers." Washington DC: US Government Printing Office.

———. 2013. "American Community Survey: Information Guide." Washington DC: US Government Printing Office.

———. 2018. "Current Population Survey, 1968–2018 Annual Social and Economic Supplements." Accessed October 18, 2020. https://www.census.gov/content/dam/Census/library/visualizations/2018/demo/p60-263/figure1.pdf.

US Office of Management and Budget. 2013. "Revised Delineations of Metropolitan Statistical Areas, Micropolitan Statistical Areas, and Combined Statistical Areas, and Guidance on Uses of the Delineations of These Areas." *OMB Bulletin No.* 13 (01).

Venkatraman, Sakshi, and P. R. Lockhart. 2020. "Not Enough or Double the Prejudice: On Being Black and Asian American in 2020." *NBC News.* Accessed October 18, 2020. https://www.nbcnews.com/news/asian-america/not-enough-or -double-prejudice-being-Black-asian-american-2020-n1243353.

Washington, Myra A. 2017. *Blasian Invasion: Racial Mixing in the Celebrity Industrial Complex.* Jackson: The University Press of Mississippi.

Waters, Mary C. 1999. *Black Identities: West Indian Immigrant Dreams and American Realities.* New York: Russell Sage Foundation.

Williams, Teresa Kay. 1992. "Prism Lives: Identity of Binational Amerasians." In *Racially Mixed People in America*, edited by Maria P. P. Root, 280–303. Newbury: Sage Publications.

Williams, Teresa Kay, and Michael C. Thornton. 1998. "Social Construction of Ethnicity Versus Personal Experience: The Case of Afro-Asians." *Journal of Comparative Family Studies* 29 (2):255–67.

Wilson, William Julius. 1980. *The Declining Significance of Race: Blacks and Changing American Institutions.* Chicago: University of Chicago Press.

Wilton, Leigh S., Diana T. Sanchez, and Julie A. Garcia. 2013. "The Stigma of Privilege: Racial Identity and Stigma Consciousness Among Biracial Individuals." *Race and Social Problems* 5:41–56.

Wooldridge, Jeffrey M. 2006. *Introductory Econometrics: A Modern Approach.* 3rd edition. Beijing: Tsinghua University Press.

Wright, Richard, Serin Houston, Mark Ellis, Steven Holloway, and Margaret Hudson. 2003. "Crossing Racial Lines: Geographies of Mixed-Race Partnering and Multiraciality in the United States." *Progress in Human Geography* 27 (4):457–74.

Xie, Yu, and Kimberly Goyette. 1997. "The Racial Identification of Biracial Children with One Asian Parent: Evidence from the 1990 Census." *Social Forces* 76 (2):547–70.

———. 2004. "A Demographic Portrait of Asian Americans." In *The American People: Census 2000*, edited by Reynolds Farley and John Haaga, 415–46. New York: Russell Sage Foundation.

Zack, Naomi. 1995. *American Mixed Race: The Culture of Microdiversity*. New York: Rowman & Littlefield.

Zhang, Yuanting, and Jennifer Van Hook. 2009. "Marital Dissolution Among Interracial Couples." *Journal of Marriage and Family* 71 (1):95–107.

Zubrinsky, Camille L., and Lawrence Bobo. 1996. "Prismatic Metropolis: Race and Residential Segregation in the City of the Angels." *Social Science Research* 25 (4):335–74.

Index

Note: Italicized pages numbers denote tables; Pages numbers followed by n denote chapter endnotes.

About the Author

Dr. **Rachel Butts** is vice president of market intelligence and research at a major financial institution. She has been working in the field of demography since 2001. A graduate of Indiana University Kelley School of Business, University of Oklahoma, and Michigan State University, Rachel wrestles with a curious mind that finds composure in unchartered territories. Rachel dwells on a small family farm in Michigan with her husband, Ryan, and daughter, Marion. She is the president of the Greater Milan Area Community Foundation and founder of the Michael A. Tittiger Sustainability & Conservation Endowment Fund, a scholarship that awards minorities interested in environmental-impact careers with college funding.

Lightning Source UK Ltd.
Milton Keynes UK
UKHW011259110621
384959UK00003B/22